BEAD LOVE

BEAD LOVE

Simply Fabulous Jewelry With Big Beautiful Beads

JANE LAFERLA

LARK BOOKS

A Division of Sterling Publishing Co., Inc.
New York

Development Editor: Terry Taylor

Art Director: Dana Irwin

Cover Designer: Barbara Zaretsky

Associate Editor: Nathalie Mornu

Associate Art Director: Lance Wille

Art Production Assistant: Jeff Hamilton

Editorial Assistance: Delores Gosnell

Editorial Intern: Megan Taylor Cox

Illustrator: Orrin Lundgren

Photographer: John Widman

Library of Congress Cataloging-in-Publication Data

LaFerla, Jane, 1949
  Bead love : simply fabulous jewelry with big beautiful beads / Jane
LaFerla.
      p. cm.
  Includes index.
  ISBN 1-57990-962-0 (hardcover)
  1. Beadwork--Patterns. 2. Jewelry making. I. Title.
  TT860.L34 2006
  745.594'2--dc22

                                                          2006020980

10 9 8 7 6 5 4 3 2 1

First Edition

Published by Lark Books, A Division of
Sterling Publishing Co., Inc.
387 Park Avenue South, New York, N.Y. 10016

Text © 2006, Lark Books
Photography © 2006, Lark Books, unless otherwise specified
Illustrations © 2006, Lark Books, unless otherwise specified

Front cover: Necklace by Susie Ragland

Distributed in Canada by Sterling Publishing,
c/o Canadian Manda Group, 165 Dufferin Street
Toronto, Ontario, Canada M6K 3H6

Distributed in the United Kingdom by GMC Distribution Services,
Castle Place, 166 High Street, Lewes, East Sussex, England BN7 1XU

Distributed in Australia by Capricorn Link (Australia) Pty Ltd.,
P.O. Box 704, Windsor, NSW 2756 Australia

If you have questions or comments about this book, please contact:
Lark Books
67 Broadway, Asheville, NC 28801
(828) 253-0467

Manufactured in China

ISBN 13: 978-157990-962-8
ISBN 10: 1-57990-962-0

For information about custom editions, special sales, premium and
corporate purchases, please contact Sterling Special Sales Department
at 800-805-5489 or specialsales@sterlingpub.com.

FOR
BEAD
LOVERS
EVERYWHERE

CONTENTS

INTRODUCTION

You want them. You know you do. Beads call your name. You hear their siren's serenade and are powerless in their presence. From the big, bad, and bodacious to mere whispers of shimmering color, they insinuate, intoxicate, insist. Sure, you call it love. But in the dark corners of your conscience lurks the realization that this craving might just be out-and-out lust.

How can you be certain? Consider these symptoms:

- You can't pass a bead shop without going in.

- You don't know what to do with the hoard of big beautiful beads you've lovingly collected over the years.

- You lapse into déjà vu whenever you look at a strand of trade beads.

- The earth moves when fistfuls of turquoise chips slip through your fingers.

If even one of these describes your behavior or makes you feel the least bit guilty, help is at hand. This book holds the key to your salvation. Thirty-seven great projects will show you how to

transform the large, luscious objects of your desire into fabulous pieces of jewelry that you can wear for all the world to see. No more lurking about, no more denial, no more excuses. Beads are no longer meant just to go *with*, they're to go *for*—and the bigger and bolder the better.

Whether your style is retro, boho, traditional, or fashion forward, you'll find necklaces, bracelets, and earrings that can mix it up with the best of them. Now is the time to get out that special bead and finally give it the recognition it deserves. The chapter on focal beads will help you take it center stage with knotted cord or interwoven strands of pearls, and will show you how to surround it with complementary beads and gems.

How about that stash of gemstones wasting away in your workshop? Set them off with silver, string them on a ribbon, or combine them to make glorious dangles and drops. From rough-cut to polished, from organic chunks of pink opal to facetted briolettes, you're sure to find designs that will turn a few heads and bring you compliments wherever you go.

If your bead collection reflects a natural bent toward materials from land and sea, you can create jewelry with beads made of bone, wood, and pearl. You can take it from ethnic to elegant it one chapter. And if funky is more your style, the chapter Glass, Plastic, and More will give you ideas galore. Designs using resin, lampwork, and even felt beads will fire your artistic imagination.

From beading wire to chain to ribbon to neoprene cord, you'll have plenty of options to inspire you when it comes to stringing. As you work with carved wooden beads, pearls, turquoise, amber, Venetian glass, raw emeralds, to name only a few, you'll fall in love all over again.

Even if you're just flirting with the idea of beads and have never made a piece of jewelry, you'll learn the techniques needed to complete every project. You'll also find interesting tidbits of bead lore, as well as a gorgeous section on contemporary artists' beads. A quick primer on design will get you started in exploring your own combinations. You can make the projects as presented here—the step-by-step instructions will tell you how—or use them as a springboard for your own creativity.

So go on, you crazy lover you. You have a pile of gorgeous beads just waiting for you. Whatever you do, silence your inner critic and follow your heart. Take a risk. Pick a project. Date it. You may find it's the start of something big. And, even after you commit beads to wire or thread, it's never too late—if you find the relationship isn't working, remember, you can always break it up and start all over again.

THE BASICS

While the art of making a fashion statement with beads is as old as humankind, the basic concept of creating beaded jewelry hasn't changed much: take a bead, string one, then another. This chapter provides a handy reference to the tools, materials, and techniques you'll need to make the projects in this book.

BEADS

Carved bone, silver Thai beads, semiprecious gem nuggets, glistening crystal, vintage plastic, artists' beads, electroformed silver—the incredible variety available today is an indication of the continued, and still growing, interest in beads. Whether you haunt the shops, go to the shows, or travel the net, beads that were once hard to find are quickly at your fingertips, and better yet, more affordable than ever.

Sizing

Beads are measured in millimeters. For those of you more accustomed to inches, the comparison chart (figure 1) should help you as you shop. You can buy beads individually or in strands. Most strands are 16 inches (40.6 cm) long, with the number of beads on each strand determined by individual size.

While the projects in this book generally use larger beads, a few projects call for seed beads. Keep in mind that seed beads have their own sizing system written as, for example, 6°, 7°, 8°, and so on—the higher the number the smaller the bead. Seed beads come in a range of colors and finishes, matte to iridescent. Delicas, with their squared cylindrical shape and large holes are approximate in size to a 12° seed bead. Bugle beads, thin hollow tubes of glass, are sized according to length with 1 being the shortest and 5 the longest.

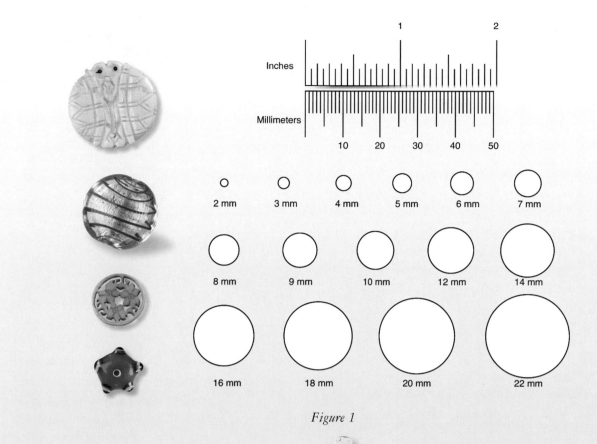

Inches

Millimeters

| | 10 | 20 | 30 | 40 | 50 |

2 mm 3 mm 4 mm 5 mm 6 mm 7 mm

8 mm 9 mm 10 mm 12 mm 14 mm

16 mm 18 mm 20 mm 22 mm

Figure 1

Bead Types

A bead type is most often defined by the material it's made from or its method of production. Sometimes a bead is even defined by its function. The more bead knowledge you accumulate, the better the outcome of your projects. Sound familiar? Like love, once you get over the initial sensory overload, it's only natural to be curious about your significant other's family and background.

Artists' beads, as the name implies, are individually crafted by artists specializing in the bead form. They can be made in a variety of media including clay, wood, paper, polymer clay, PMC, cloisonné enamel, and precious metal. For more on contemporary artists' beads, see page 30.

Bone beads can be made from the bones of yaks, camels, cattle, or goats. The material provides a perfect medium for carving, incising designs, and painting or dyeing.

Crystal beads are made from leaded glass. They can be clear or colored and are easily faceted, which gives them their lovely light-reflective quality. Mostly manufactured in uniform shapes and sizes, they are readily available.

Glass beads come in almost endless varieties. Whatever can be done to form glass can be employed to make beads. Lovely hand-blown Venetian-glass beads or millefiori caned beads are beautiful to behold. Standard shapes, such as circles or ovals, and surface treatments, such as faceted or smooth, can be found wherever beads are sold. Pressing glass allows different shapes to emerge, such as shells, leaves, and imprinted medallions. Because pressed-glass beads have been traditionally made in the Czech Republic, they are commonly called Czech glass.

Dichroic glass beads, with their multihued, iridescent surfaces, are made by applying thin layers of metallic oxides to the glass, which is then fired at high temperatures.

Lampwork beads, created by bead artists specializing in the technique, are made by working hot glass rods over a flame. Once made using the flame of a lamp, hence the name, today most artists work over a propane torch. Lampwork beads are known for their wonderful colors and the interesting swirls and dots of glass that texture their surfaces.

Metal beads can be made of any metal that will hold its shape, including base metal, silver, gold, aluminum, steel, copper, lead-free pewter, and brass. Base metal can be electroplated with silver or gold to simulate the look of solid precious metals. Sterling silver that has been electroplated with

gold is called vermeil. Some silver beads take common names from the country or locale where they were originally crafted, such as Bali beads, Thai silver, and hill tribe beads. Electroformed beads, made by depositing a fine layer of sterling silver or gold on a wax form, are lightweight and economical to use.

Polymer clay beads are modeled, much like clay, into various shapes. The properties of this material allow artists to make lightweight beads. The designs can range from simulated marble or semiprecious stones to colorful flights of fantasy.

Precious Metal Clay (PMC) is a cousin to polymer clay. Finely ground particles of silver or gold are bound to a malleable substance. After modeling, the clay is heated, which allows the substance to disintegrate and the metal particles to fuse, leaving a solid metal object. Though often used for artists' beads, one-of-a-kind findings are also made from PMC.

Resin and plastic beads offer a contemporary option when choosing beads. Their translucent surfaces in appealing, bright colors look as good with silver as they do with neoprene cord.

Semiprecious stone beads are a bountiful gift from mother nature. Whether left in their organic shape or cut and polished, they present a beauty all their own. From pearls to jasper, amber to turquoise, fluorite to jade, you'll find colors and textures to inspire any design. Use this color list for semiprecious stones as quick reference when planning a design.

SEMIPRECIOUS STONE BEADS

Black/Gray—black agate, black jade, hematite, labradorite (with play of color), manganite, pearl, smoky quartz, tektite

Blue—amazonite, aquamarine, azurite, barite, benitoite, fluorite, heliodor, kyanite, lapis lazuli, lazulite, turquoise

Green—amazonite, chrysoprase, demantoid, diopside, dioptase, enstatite, green jade, hiddenite, malachite, moss agate, olivenite, peridot, prasiolite, sphene, turquoise, uvarovite

Red/Pink—coral, cornelian, rodochrosite, rose quartz, scapolite, some garnets

Yellow/Orange—amber, amblygonite, anatase, andalusite, citrine, marchasite, orpiment, orthoclase, phenacite, pryrite

Brown—fossilized wood or animal matter, sard, spessartite, tiger's eye

Purple—amethyst, tanzanite

White/Milky—coral, hambergite, moonstone, opal (with play of color), pearl

Spacer beads are the unsung heroes of the bead world. They rarely take center stage, but are always content to just string along. As their name implies, they fill spaces between beads. But design-wise they're much more. Sometimes they act as a visual pause, like a punctuation mark in poetry. At other times, they provide the harmony to the dominant beads' melody line. No matter how you look at them, always consider them an integral part of your design.

Vintage beads can be purchased separately or can be taken from old necklaces to be recycled into new designs. Hunting beads in secondhand stores is not only fun, it can yield unique finds that are also economical.

Bead Shapes

Bead shapes are, for the most part, descriptive. Like learning a language, once you know the names of the basic shapes it's easy to add adjectives to them that any beader will understand. Take a rectangle, for instance. That pretty much describes the basic shape, but a flat rectangle is another shape altogether, and if you put faceted in the mix, a faceted flat rectangle takes it to another level. Here is a list of some of the shapes you're likely to encounter. Most of the shape names are self-explanatory; if not, a short description follows them.

Almond

Arrowhead

Axe head—fan shaped or one-quarter of a circle

Barrel

Bicone—two cones fused end to end

Bowtie

Branch—organically shaped, cropped frangia

Brick

Briolette—pear-shaped with triangular facets

Bugle—cylinder with larger piercing

Button—any shape slightly puffed or domed

Capsule

Cathedral—stepped ends with a faceted ring around the middle

Chevron—wide V-shape

Chip—roughly cut chunks

Coin

Cone

Crow—traditional rounded beads with large holes, similar to pony beads, but bigger

Cube

Cupolini—polished chips that are shaped, sized, and grouped accordingly

Curved tube

Cushion—puffed square, sometimes nicknamed a squoval

Cylinder

Diamond

Die—side-drilled cube

Disk—a slice of a cylinder

Domed—any geometric shape with curvilinear sides

Donut—any shape with an equilateral cutout that mimics the perimeter shape

Dotted lines—round pony beads with ridges formed by lines of dots

Double tube—tube with another shorter tube layered around it

Drop—fattened teardrop

Druk—to the eye, perfectly round glass beads sans seam lines

Drum—can have straight sides or curved sides to resemble an hourglass

Ellipse

Faced round—small round bead with six flattened faces

Faceted—any shape where curved lines have been squared off into facets (e.g., faceted cone, faceted oval)

Fan

Filigree—a hollow bead with a decorative network of surface lines

Flat

Flat-sided—any shape pressed into a flat shape (i.e., flat heart vs. puffed heart)

Flatter cube—traditional cube with flattened edges that make extra facets

Frangia—Italian for fringe, are groupings of long branched beads

Freeform—anything goes

Go-go—round off-center donut; also called magatama

Hair pipe—extremely elongated bicone

Heart

Heishi—denotes disks cut from shell

Hex rondelle—rondelle with six faceted sides

Leaf

Lentil

Long drop—pierced from tip to tip rather than across the top

Marquise—low pointed oval, as in a marquise-cut gem

Melon—a fat round bead with rounded ridges (or cast lines) mimicking melon skin

Mosaic—smaller barrels with rounded ends

Nugget—organically shaped lump

Oval

Peanut

Pear

Pebble—a pinched oval

Points—organically shaped, resembling a long crystal

Polygon—twelve flat faces

Pony—traditional rounded beads with large holes, similar to crow beads, but smaller

Puffed—fattened, softened version of original shape (e.g., puffed rectangle, puffed disk, etc.)

Pumpkin

Pyramid—square base with triangular sides

Rectangle

Rice

Rococo—organically shaped, mostly denotes pearls that are flat on one end

Rondelle—flat and circular

Round

Rounded drop—highly faceted narrow drop with points more rounded than sharp

Saucer

Sharp drop—drop cut so all facets join at a common, prominent point

Shield—slightly curvilinear triangle

Slab

Spindle—resembles a fused set of graduated rondelle beads

Square

Squared tube—squared cylinder with rounded corners and ends

Star

Starflake—a six-pointed snowflake that can interlock with others

Stick—as a group, denotes pearls that are long and flattened, also known as baroque

Tablet—elongated puffed rectangle with rounded edges

Teardrop

Triangle

Tribead—three nodules extending from a common pierced center, each bead can interlock with other tribeads

Trumpet—uniformly ridged cone with wide flare at one end

Tube

Twist—any shape twisted half to full turn

Vase—a traditional round bead with a ring of glass around each end piercing

Wheel—basic wheel shape with diamond-faceted outward-facing sides

TOOLS AND MATERIALS

Imagine. With a few simple tools and basic jewelry-making materials, you can transform the beads you love into that necklace or bracelet you adore. In fact, you could be wearing it tonight.

Basic Tools

For most projects, you'll use pliers and cutters—how easy is that? You may find a few other tools helpful. But if you don't have them, you can improvise to get the same results.

Chain-nose pliers easily maneuver through links of chain. Their tapered jaws are rounded on the outside, flat on the inside.

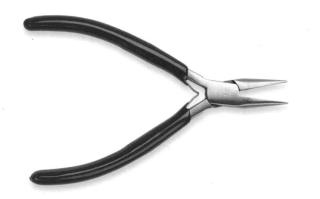

Crimping pliers easily secure wire or thread with a crimp bead. They have two sets of notches on their jaws; one to crush the crimp and the other to shape it. While you can use almost any pair of pliers to crush a crimp, crimping pliers offer the convenience of using one tool for the job.

Flat-nose pliers securely hold wire in their flat, squared jaws when wrapping or pulling beading wire to tighten it.

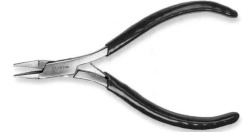

Needle-nose pliers are similar to chain nose-pliers, but have even longer tapered jaws. You can use them when making wrapped loops, for shaping wire, or when attaching crimps (see Crimp beads on page 21).

Round-nose pliers, with their tapered, round jaws, shape wire and are essential for making simple and wrapped loops used for attaching beads.

Pliers have either serrated or smooth surfaces on their jaws. Smooth-jawed pliers are preferable for jewelry making since they will not scratch the materials you use. If you're going to invest in a set of pliers, make sure they're smooth jawed. If you want to use the serrated pliers you already have, you can wrap the jaws with surgical adhesive tape to protect your work—just be careful to avoid getting any of the adhesive on your materials.

Wire cutters need to cut flush to avoid pesky bits of wire—known as burrs—that can scrape skin or catch on clothing.

Bead boards allow you to organize and lay out beads for your design while helping you measure length with precision. They're inexpensive but not indispensable. You can also purchase velvety bead mats, which are soft and come in different colors. Or in a pinch, you can lay your beads out on a towel to prevent them from rolling as you work.

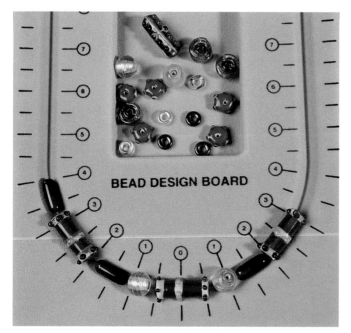

Beading needles for stringing beads with small holes or for weaving come in different sizes; the larger the number, the bigger the needle. For stringing larger beads, twisted-wire needles with big eyes are easy to use and thread.

Chasing hammer and jeweler's block are useful when shaping or tempering metal. If you don't have either, you can substitute by using a small metal hammer on a solid surface.

Clips are like an extra pair of hands. They help keep your work together when you need to move to another task. Small alligator clips found in electronics stores are perfect for beading.

Mandrels are straight or tapered rods that are used for shaping wire. If you don't have a mandrel you can improvise by using a wooden dowel or the round handle on a file.

Small motorized craft tools or electric bead reamers with diamond-tip drill bits are especially helpful when you need to enlarge the holes of stone beads.

Occasionally you'll get a stone bead with a hole that's too small to pass through your wire or needle. Enlarging the hole with a small motorized craft tool or electric bead reamer will soon get you back to work. A .75 mm diamond-tip drill bit will work for most beads. Before you begin drilling, secure the bead, then use short strokes until the hole is the right size. To avoid unbalancing the bead, make sure you drill from both sides.

Stringing Materials

Choosing the right stringing material is crucial to the success of your project. You'll need stronger, thicker thread or wire if you're working with heavy beads. And you'll need materials that won't fray when working with cut-glass beads with sharp corners or stones that have holes with rough edges.

Beading thread and cord can be made of polyamid, synthetic fibers, cotton, or silk. Make sure to use the appropriate size and type of thread for the beads in your design.

Chain, with links of varying shapes and sizes, allows you infinite design possibilities. You can attach beads to dangle off the links, or you can open the links and attach beads or groupings of beads to them using simple or wrapped-wire loops.

Decorative cords beg to be seen. Their interesting variety of textures fit any design from primitive to ultra modern, from romantic to rustic. They include ribbon, leather, silk cord, waxed linen, hemp cord, neoprene cord, and artificial sinew.

Elastic beading cord is perfect for creating quick to make and wear bracelets.

Glue keeps knots from unraveling. You can also use clear nail polish remover. On decorative cords that can't be knotted or twisted, such as leather and neoprene, you will need to use two-part epoxy to attach findings for a finished look.

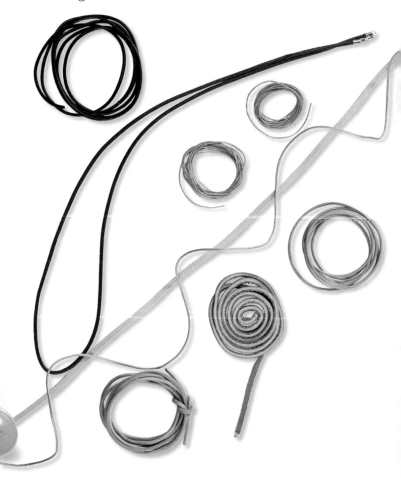

Flexible beading wire is known under many brand names, but its basic structure is the same. Multistrands of steel are bundled together, then coated in nylon to create a wire that is strong and flexible. Wire can be made from bundles of 7, 19, or 49 strands. Some wire is coated with colored nylon, giving you options for your design palette; others are coated with clear nylon when you prefer having the color of the metal show through. Wire comes in different diameters ranging from .010 to .030 inches (.250 to .760mm).

Neck wires for making necklaces are premeasured, shaped wires ready for stringing. They can be made of smooth wire or cable, and come with attached clasps of different types. Neck wires can be gold-filled or made of gold or sterling silver.

Wire comes in different shapes and gauges. The lower the number the thicker the wire—14-gauge wire is much thicker than 24-gauge. You may notice the terms dead soft or half-hard when shopping for wire. They describe the degree of softness of the wire, which tells you how flexible it is. Wire becomes harder as you work with it. If your wire is too soft, you can harden it by tapping it gently with a chasing hammer on a jeweler's block, or with a small hammer on a solid surface.

Findings

These manufactured jewelry components help you keep it all together. They're little bits of heroic hardware that hold, attach, link, or close your beaded projects while giving them a professional finish.

Bead caps fit over the tops and bottoms of beads. Their resemblance to little caps says it all. They're used to finish a strand of beads or as spacers between beads.

Bead tips finish single-strand pieces strung on thread. Shaped like partial, hollow beads with a hook on the end, they provide a hiding space for knots at the end of a strand, and the means for attaching the strand to a finding.

Clasps can accommodate one strand or many. They can be as uncomplicated as hooks and eyes, or have simple spring mechanisms for extra safety. Toggle clasps have a bar side and a ring side. S-hooks look like their namesake and do well with heavy beads. Lobster clasps resemble a lobster claw and have a spring catch for securing delicate beads. It's important to chose your clasp with as much care

as you do your beads to complement the design. Besides fabricated clasps that you can find in stores and catalogues, look for handcrafted clasps that will bring your jewelry to beautiful closure.

Cones make an attractive finishing touch for multi-strand necklaces. To use them, join the strands by attaching them to a common loop on a length of wire, then thread the wire through the cone. To attach a clasp, make a loop on the wire tail coming from the cone.

Crimp beads secure the ends of beading wire to keep the beads on while providing a means for attaching a clasp. As shown in figure 2, string a crimp bead on the wire, loop the wire through the clasp, then pass it back through the crimp bead. Use chain-nose, needle-nose, or crimping pliers to snug the crimp bead close to the clasp and the last bead on the strand before using the pliers to flatten the crimp. The advantage to using crimping pliers (see page 16) is their notched jaws were specially designed to handle this one task.

Figure 2

Earring wires, posts, and clips all have one thing in common—a point of attachment on which you can hang your beads. You want to choose earring findings that are comfortable and complement your design. However, be aware you want to choose findings that will accommodate the weight of the beads you'll be using. Beads that are too heavy for the finding won't hang properly and run the risk of slipping out of the ear. Using ear wires with a fastening reduces this risk.

End caps allow you to finish non-metal cords such as leather, rubber, plastic, and neoprene. You attach them to the cords using two-part epoxy.

Head pins and eye pins are short lengths of wire used for stringing beads. Head pins have one flattened or decorative end that acts as a stop for the beads. Eye pins have loops at the bottom, which stop the beads and allow you to attach more beads or charms. The wire tail of a head or eye pin can be shaped into a loop (see Making a Simple Loop on page 24 and Making a Wrapped Loop on page 25), giving them a point of attachment.

Jump rings are circles of wire that are cut somewhere on their circumference, which allows you to open and close them. Since you use them to attach components, you want them to remain strong. Opening jump rings by spreading the ends apart will weaken the metal. The correct way to open and close them is to use two pliers to twist the ends, bringing one forward and the other back, as shown in figure 3.

Spacers are rigid bars with two to five holes that separate and keep multiple strands in order.

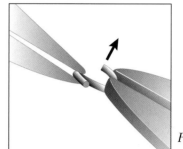

Figure 3

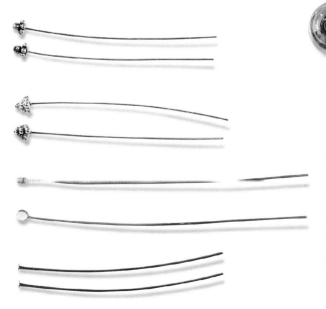

TECHNIQUES

Most of the techniques you need to know have one purpose—how to assemble your beads into a luscious whole. Whether you need to attach them to each other, to various components of the design, or to their findings, these techniques are all about making the right connections.

Knots

Once reserved as a technique for stringing precious pearls, using knots to separate beads offers many options for contemporary design. When using decorative cord or ribbon, knots allow you to space the beads to your liking. An overhand knot is all you need, but you want to make sure you snug the knot close to the bead. Using beading tweezers will help.

1. While holding the bead to be tied, make the knot with your fingers, drawing it fairly close to the bead, but do not tighten it.

2. Place the tweezers through the knot and pinch the cord close to the place where the knot will end. Then draw the cord taut as you slip the knot tighter around the tweezers.

3. When you're close to the final tightening, keep pinching the cord as you slip the tweezers out, then slip the knot as close and tight as you can to the bead. While making the knots and pulling the cord, watch the free end of the cord to make sure it doesn't make a pesky secondary knot.

Making a Simple Loop

Open the loop, attach it, then close it up. A simple loop is as easy to make as it is to use.

1. As shown in figure 4, use pliers to bend the end of the wire 90° to make a right angle, leaving enough wire at the end to make a loop.

2. Using your round-nose pliers, grasp the wire close to the bend of the angle, then roll the pliers to shape the loop. If needed, use wire cutters to trim any excess wire.

3. The finished loop is ready for attachment. Once it's in place, gently squeeze the loop with pliers to secure it.

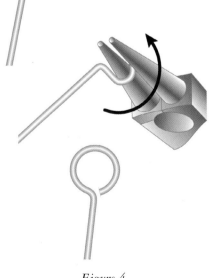

Figure 4

Making a Wrapped Loop

A wrapped loop provides an extra measure of security when attaching beads while providing a decorative twist. You can make them on one end of a wire or head pin after threading your beads. Or, you can make them on both ends of a length of wire after threading your beads, which will allow you to attach the beads to other components of your design.

1. As shown in figure 5, use needle-nose or chain-nose pliers to bend the wire 90° to make a right angle. Leave enough distance between the bend of the angle and the last bead to allow for two to three wraps of wire.

2. As you did for Making a Simple Loop on page 24, use your round-nose pliers to grasp the wire close to the bend of the right angle, then roll the pliers to shape the loop. Remove the pliers from the loop and reinsert them with the lower jaw inside the loop. Use your hands to wrap the wire around the pliers. Do not trim the wire.

3. Make sure the loop is upright, then grasp it with your needle-nose or chain-nose pliers. Using your hands, and keeping the wire at a right angle as you work, wrap the wire tail around the neck of the wire.

4. Continue wrapping until you are almost to the top of the bead, cut the wire, then tuck the end close to the remaining length.

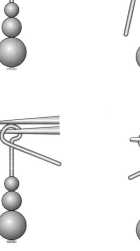

Figure 5

Oxidizing

When you want metal to take on an aged patina, you will use an oxidizing preparation. It darkens the metal's surface, which allows you to remove as much of the oxidation as you desire to create the effect you seek. Though there are several commercial preparations, liver of sulphur remains the jewelers' favorite. To use it, dissolve it in hot water, submerging the metal you want oxidized in the solution. Remove the metal, dry it, then use 0000 steel wool to remove as much of the oxidation as you want and to polish the metal. When using commercial preparations, always follow the manufacturer's instructions.

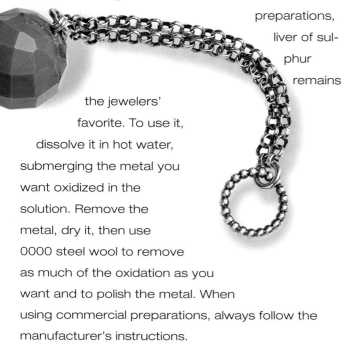

DESIGN AND COLOR

How do you, the bead lover, approach design when you want to make nothing less than a knock-out piece? If you're at a loss for ideas, let the beads tell you. Okay, that may sound a bit too weird, but it's not as strange as you think. There had to be that special something that attracted you to them in the first place—and getting back to that moment can be one of your richest sources of inspiration.

Ask yourself exactly what it was about the beads that grabbed your attention? Was it the bold lines, the organic shapes, the bright colors, or the swirling patterns in the glass? Looking at the words you use to describe the beads can help you focus your thoughts. In this example, each word—bold, organic, bright, or swirling—represents a design concept with dozens of possibilities. And all you have to do is choose one. Now it's time to play.

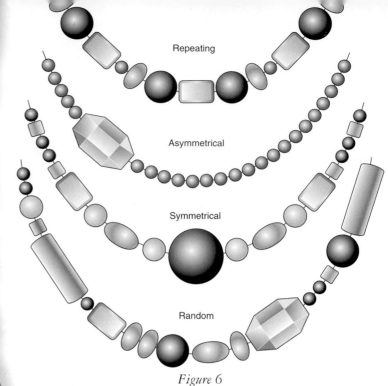

Repeating

Asymmetrical

Symmetrical

Random

Figure 6

Take Time to Plan

One of the hardest steps in beading is making your-self take the time to develop a plan. Who can blame you? When faced with an array of beautiful beads all you want to do is get to work. However, just think of planning as more fun time you can spend with your beads. Use a bead board (see page 17) or lay them out on a towel so they won't roll around. Place differ-ent types and colors of spacer beads between the larger beads. Experiment with some common designs, as shown in figure 6. Arrange and rearrange to your heart's content until you have a design you can't live without.

Although a repeating pattern may sound boring, it's anything but. It's one of the best ways to combine colors and textures with ease. The eye quickly picks up on the pattern and is reassured by it. An asym-metrical design is a wonderful way to give a bit of extra emphasis to a focal bead since the eye will hunt for it when it's placed off center.

Try a symmetrical design when working with unusual beads. This more formal arrangement will juxtapose with their quirky qualities to highlight them even more. Random design allows you the most freedom. You can mix and layer textures, or stick to one. You can vary the size of the beads or keep them perfectly in proportion to one another.

As you design, keep in mind who will be wearing the jewelry. A long necklace with large beads will look odd on a short person, and a delicate choker might be all wrong for someone who is tall or large. Other considerations would be face shape, the length of a person's neck, or the size of their wrist. Also what does the person usually wear? It would be useless to make a necklace that would look great with a deep V neckline if the person only wears turtlenecks. You want to make sure a necklace is comfortable to wear as well. While you may love using large nuggets, the weight of using too many might keep the necklace from being worn.

Length

Know to what lengths you're willing to go. If you're making a necklace, do you want it to be a demure choker, a pretty princess, or a dramatic rope? The common lengths, as shown in figure 7, have names.

Choker, 15 to 16 inches (38. 5 to 41 cm)

Princess, 18 inches (46 cm)

Matinee, 20 to 26 inches (51 to 67 cm)

Opera, 28 to 36 inches (72 to 91.5 cm)

Rope (or Lariat), 48 inches (123.5 cm)

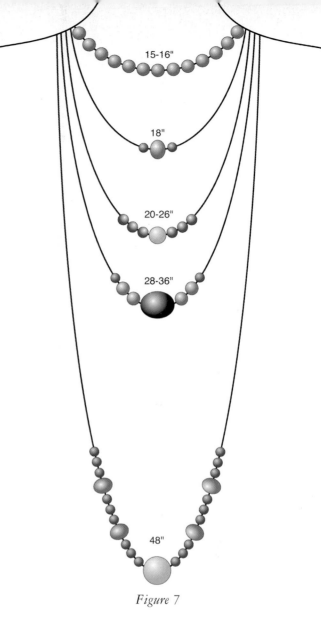

Figure 7

Color

When it comes to choosing color, search your memory for tips you might remember from Art 101. Find a color wheel and take it for a spin. Monochromatic? Definitely dramatic. Complementary colors? Opposites attract. Cool? And contained. Warm? Sunny disposition. Mix it up by using secondary colors. Meet the analogous neighbors, or keep it all in the family. Allow yourself to experiment with color combinations that are out of your comfort zone. Try making your favorite outfit be your inspiration—even if it's black and white.

ARTISTS'

At a time when most beads are machine-made, some contemporary artists are creating handmade beads from a wide range of materials including paper and glass. These one-of-a-kind beads can inspire you to create a special piece of jewelry. In a way, it's as if you're collaborating with the bead artist to carry on the creative process begun when the bead was made. Look for artists' beads in galleries, local bead shops, or at craft fairs.

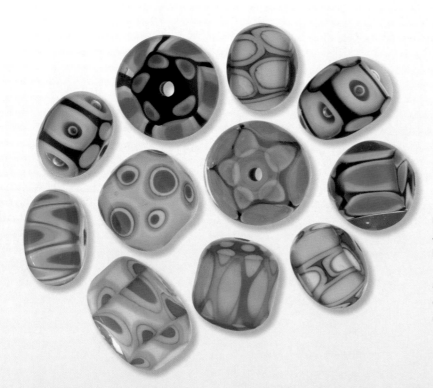

DEBBY YABCZANKA
Summer Collection, 2006
Largest bead, 11/16 x 11/16 x 1/2 inch
(1.7 x 1.3 cm)
Soda-lime glass; flameworked,
encased, plunged dots
PHOTO BY JIM SWALLOW

DEBBY YABCZANKA has been making glass beads since 1999. After discovering that a friend made her own glass beads, an intrigued Debby learned the basics of flameworking in a few hours and became hooked on making the candy-like drops. She relishes finding new possibilities for combining mouth-watering colors and shaping glass, and enjoys the challenge of making multiples of the same size and design. A designer has used her beads as buttons in several clothing collections. Debby combines her beads with sterling silver elements to make bracelets, necklaces, and earrings.

BEADS

HADAR JACOBSON became curious about precious metal clay shortly after its introduction about a decade ago. "I thought it might be the answer to my love for textures," she says. Hadar bought a kiln and taught herself to use the material by trial and error. Now an expert, she says the hardest part of working with metal clay is trying to prevent the hollow forms from collapsing during firing. She generally strings her beads on necklaces and bracelets.

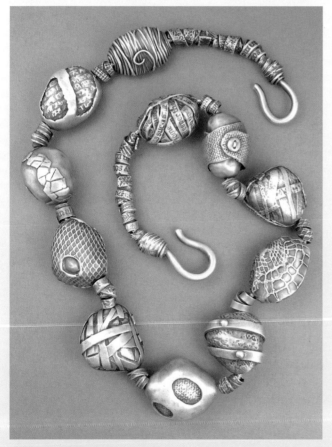

HADAR JACOBSON
Eleven Rocks, 2004
Largest bead, 13/16 x 7/16 x 7/16 inch (2 x 1 x 1 cm)
Hollow-formed metal clay, fine silver; hand fabricated, fired, oxidized
PHOTO BY ARTIST

BRONWYNN LUSTED
Untitled, 2006
Largest bead, 2⅛ inch (5.4 cm) in diameter
Clockwise from left, Tasmanian blackwood, padauk, orange cankerberry and beneath it ebony, wenge, gidgee
PHOTO BY JOHN WIDMAN

BRONWYNN LUSTED doesn't own or sport any jewelry, though she loves making it, and is glad other women like wearing her designs. She crafts substantial beads from various woods—both soft and hard—and from burls, seed pods, and nuts. She uses wood that is salvaged, purchased, or collected from her property in the Australian bush. Bronwynn's husband taught her to work with wood, and the word "passionate" doesn't adequately describe her devotion to her craft. "Every minute of the day spent on cooking, washing, or cleaning is wasted time that could have been spent making beads," she says.

GWEN L. FISHER makes beads from other beads. After admiring beading in a shop window, Gwen used *The Art and Elegance of Beadweaving*, by Carol Wilcox Wells, as her textbook to learn the stitches, then quickly moved on to designing her own pieces. With needle and thread, she weaves seed beads into larger beads. "It's easy to sew a bunch of beads together to make a wad of beads and thread," Gwen cautions. "It's a whole different task to make that wad look aesthetically pleasing." Gwen calls her beads that are too big for wearing—spheres five centimeters in diameter—golf balls, or objets d'art. She and fellow beader and friend Florence Turnour inspire each other. You can admire their work at www.beadinfinitum.com.

KAREN LEWIS, aka Klew, has used polymer clay to fashion beads for two decades. She uses it to make necklaces, key fobs, earrings, boxes, money clips, and votive holders. One day, sitting in her studio with close friends, she dropped a piece of pre-shaped bead on the floor, but decided to pick it up later. "The conversation in the room was deep in nature," she recalls, "with the friends contemplating being present in order to allow the process of creation to reveal itself." Klew later discovered the dropped bead stuck in the pattern of her sole, with a bit of wire embedded into it. "At first I was disappointed," she says. "Then the afternoon's conversation flooded my mind. I now have a bead in my line called 'Allowing the Process' and it's one of my best sellers!"

KAREN LEWIS ᴀᴋᴀ **KLEW**
Accent Beads, 2005
Largest bead, ¾ x ¾ x ½ inch
(1.9 x 1.9 x 1.3 cm)
Polymer clay
PHOTO BY MARCIA ALBREIT

LAURENCE MENHINICK, a French transplant to England, has used friction for the past few years to transform colorful wool into playful felt beads. "Since you shape them between your hands, your palms can get quite hot," she says. Laurence derives her greatest satisfaction from embellishing and shaping her beads through a number of methods—by needle felting, applying thread or glass beads, or by cutting the felt to reveal interior colors and patterns. Laurence points out that though the beads work well for necklaces, bracelets, and fashion accessories, they can also be used alone or in clusters to embellish items such as handbags, belts, cushions, hats, embroideries, etc. "They're so light, anything goes!" she says.

LAURENCE MENHINICK
Untitled, 2005–2006
Largest bead, 1¼ inches (3.2 cm) in diameter
Merino wool, embroidery floss, sequins,
seed beads; felted
PHOTO BY JOHN WIDMAN

JOAN MILLER
From left to right, *Heart Round*,
Hearts + Flowers Large Hollow;
Bicone, and two untitled beads, 2006
Largest bead, 1⅛ x 1 x ⅝ inch
(3 x 2.5 x 1.5 cm)
Colored porcelain, clear glaze
PHOTO BY JOHN WIDMAN

JOAN MILLER has made her ornamented, porcelain beads with intricate—and miniscule—detail since taking a pottery course at Baltimore Clayworks in 1988. Even though she had worked with clay before, at that moment the timing happened to be perfect. Her pursuit of the art bead was inspired by lampworking. "I picked up the general technique of working with colored slips (liquid clay) and have developed my own repertoire of tricks over the years," she says. "I think the challenge is to think of the bead as an individual work of art and a component at the same time."

MIRJAM NORINDER from Sweden rolls paper beads from the pages of newspaper and telephone directories. "I like the spool shape of the paper bead," she says, "and how it works like a reservoir for words and numbers." She's been making paper beads for years, but doesn't recall where she picked up the skill. "As a child I tried unsuccessfully to roll beads out of glossy magazines," she remembers. These days, Mirjam says the greatest hurdle to rolling a large paper bead is controlling the color, curves, and volume. She creates beads specifically for her own jewelry designs, such as brooches, bracelets, or rings like the one pictured.

MIRJAM NORINDER
Untitled, 2003
Largest bead,
approximately ⅜ inch
(1 cm)
Rolled newspaper, silver
PHOTO BY ARTIST

BARBARA MINOR enamels on copper, silver, and gold. Not only do the lustrous beads feel good to hold, she says, but they're wearable, with the added interest of glossy patterns of color. Barbara studied metalsmithing while getting her bachelor's degree, then began enameling in graduate school, but her enamel beads are the product of independent research. Many of the beads grace necklaces. They're assembled on special cables, developed by her husband, Christopher Hentz, that maintain a graceful, circular line around the neck rather than drooping to a V. Barbara also creates earrings, cuff links, rings, and brooches from her beads.

BARBARA MINOR WITH CHRISTOPHER HENTZ
Spool Bead Grouping, 2004
Largest bead, 1½ x 1 inch
(3.8 x 2.5 cm) in diameter
Transparent enamel, 24-karat gold foil, fine silver foil, fine silver, sterling silver; fabricated, micro-chased
PHOTO BY RALPH GABRINER

KATHIE MURPHY is an authority on polyester resin, and has written a book on making jewelry from it. The British artist began working with resin in 1995, and describes it as a versatile, tactile material that takes color and texture easily.

KATHIE MURPHY
Necklace, 2004
Largest bead,
2.5 x 0.7 cm
Polyester resin, thread
PHOTO BY ARTIST

CORINNE FLOYD
Unidirectional Beads, 2004
Largest bead, ⅜ x ⅜ x ⅜ inch
(1 x 1 x 1 cm) 22-karat gold
bi-metal, sterling silver; hand
fabricated, hollow construction
PHOTO BY JEFF SCOVIL

Corinne Floyd has worked with metal for more than a decade. Her
restrained trillion-shaped beads are formed and soldered sterling silver with a single 22-karat gold bimetal face. Her aim was to join the
beads to create a contemporary neckpiece with a unidirectional
look. The first item Corinne created using these beads won first
place in the necklace division of the 2004
Lapidary Journal Bead Arts Awards.

F CAL
BEADS

Focal beads
need no
introduction.
You know them
when you see them.
Big,
bold, or
bright, they
beg to become the
centerpiece of any
design.

DESIGNER: DARLENE ROGALSKI

Three largest beads by Dave Jaggers; Sterling silver PMC toggle by Zoa Art

ART GLASS BEAD BRACELET

This bracelet proves that, with art, you can never have too much of a good thing. Every element, from lampwork beads to handcrafted toggle, works beautifully together. So what's the secret to this masterpiece? Using a small black rondelle between the artists' beads allows each color to be seen without competition from neighboring bright colors.

WHAT YOU NEED

Artists' lampwork beads

Blackstone rondelles

2 sterling silver 2 x 2mm crimp beads

Handcrafted PMC toggle clasp

10 inches (25.5 cm), approximately, of flexible 49-strand beading wire

Flat-nose jewelry pliers

Wire cutters

Finished length: 7 inches (17.8 cm)

INSTRUCTIONS

1. Under a good light, which will better enable you to see the color combinations, lay the beads on a black velvet pad or soft, dark surface. Try to break up the pattern here and there. Notice how placing two similar beads next to each other (the two pink beads) between the two larger flat beads creates an unexpected grouping.

2. Since this bracelet uses a toggle clasp, plan to string smaller beads with flat ends next to the toggle. If you use larger round beads, you may have a hard time inserting the toggle bar into the ring.

3. Once you have established the stringing pattern, begin by threading on a crimp bead, and positioning it approximately 1 inch (2.5 cm) from the end. Loop the wire through one side of the toggle and back through the crimp. Use the flat-nose pliers to crush the crimp. As you thread the first bead, make sure it hides the end of the wire.

4. Thread the remaining beads, placing one of the small black rondelles between each of the larger beads. End with a crimp bead, loop the wire through the other side of the toggle, and pass the thread back through the crimp and a few of the beads. Use the flat-nose pliers to pull the wire tail tight to avoid leaving any slack before crushing the crimp. Use the wire cutters to trim any excess wire.

VENETIAN DREAMS

Who hasn't gone to Venice and fallen in love—with the incredible glass work, that is. The designer brought the hollow focus bead back from her travels and transformed it into a dream of a necklace. The aquamarine and citrine play off the light of the large bead like sunlight on the canals.

WHAT YOU NEED

1 fabulous hollow glass bead

1 oval 10mm citrine

36 round 4mm citrines

18-inch (45.7 cm) strand (or longer) of small aquamarine buttons

1 decorative gold bead cap

2 gold crimp beads

2 gold jump rings

Gold S-hook clasp

Flexible beading wire

20 to 24 inches (50.8 to 61 cm) of gold chain

24- to 28-gauge gold wire

Flat-nose pliers

Wire cutters

Round-nose pliers

Finished length: 24 inches (61 cm), including focal bead and chain fringe

INSTRUCTIONS

1. Cut three lengths of chain for the fringe that will fall from the focal bead. Cut them between 3 and 5 inches (7.6 and 12.7 cm) long, depending on the length of fringe you desire.

2. Cut a 4-inch (10.2 cm) length of gold wire, and string the last link of each of the chain lengths onto it. Use the round-nose pliers to make a loop from which the chains will dangle. Trim any excess wire.

3. String a bead cap on the wire with its cup facing down (inverted), then the focal bead, and finally the oval citrine. Using the round-nose pliers, make a wrapped loop at the top of the wire.

4. Decide how long you want the necklace. Note: Making the strands at least 18 to 22 inches (45.7 to 55.9 cm) long creates a more dramatic setting for larger focus beads.

5. Cut the rest of the chain into 1-inch (2.5 cm) lengths. For now, cut only a few lengths, cutting more as you work. Cut lengths of gold wire long enough to string three citrines and make wrapped loops at both ends.

6. Thread a length of the gold wire through the last link of one 1-inch (2.5 cm) section of chain, and make a wrapped loop with the round-nose pliers. String three of the 4mm citrines on the wire, attaching the other end of the wire to another section of chain using a wrapped loop. Continue in this way, alternating sections of chain with three strung citrines, until you have a length of fancy chain approximately ½ to 1 inch (1.3 to 2.5 cm) shorter than the desired length of necklace.

7. Fold the beaded chain in half to determine which link of chain is the center point. Using round-nose pliers, attach that link to the wrapped loop at the top of the large bead assembly.

8. String the flexible beading wire through the loop of the large bead assembly. String equal lengths of aquamarine buttons on either side of it until you've reached the desired length of your necklace.

9. String the ends of the beading wire through the last link of chain on each side of the necklace. Then string on a crimp bead, then a jump ring. String the beading wire back through the crimp bead. Using the flat-nose pliers, pull the beading wire tight, then use the pliers to crush the crimp. Fasten the ends of the S-hook clasp to the jump rings.

DESIGNER: CYNTHIA MCEWEN

Focal bead by Cynthia McEwen

THREE-STRAND CINDERELLA NECKLACE

No ugly stepsisters here—this is definitely Cinderella happily ever after. The lovely selection of pearls, vermeil, and accent beads play off, and support the design of the central lampwork bead, keeping it forever in focus.

BEAD LOVE

WHAT YOU NEED

1½-inch (4 cm) long lampwork focal bead

Assorted 4 to 6mm accent beads

8° seed beads in three coordinating colors

34 (approximately) 4 to 5mm pearls in three different colors

16 (approximately) vermeil beads in three different styles

12 2mm crimp tubes

1 vermeil toggle clasp

3 strands of flexible beading wire, each 23 inches (58.4 cm) long

Tiny flat clamps

Crimping pliers

Wire cutters

Finished length: 18 inches (45.7 cm)

INSTRUCTIONS

1. To give the necklace a strong focal point, you want to highlight the large bead with the right accent beads. String the focal bead first on one strand of wire, then choose beads that will be on either side. You may want to try different combinations of accent beads until you are satisfied.

2. Using the seed beads and approximately one-sixth of the pearls, vermeil, and assorted accent beads, randomly string approximately a 6½-inch (16.5 cm) length off one side of the focal bead and accents. On the next 1 inch (2.5 cm) of wire, string a crimp tube and a few more seed beads with holes large enough to accommodate three strands of wire. String another crimp tube and a large vermeil bead, which will be next to the toggle clasp and will cluster the three strands together.

3. String the wire through the loop on one side of the toggle, then string back through the seed beads, the two crimps, and a couple more beads. Use a tiny clamp to hold the beads to the wire while you work on the other side.

4. Repeat steps 2 and 3 on the other side of the focal bead. Check your length. Be sure the focal bead hangs in the center. Adjust accordingly. Remove the clamps. Use the crimping pliers, crimp all crimp beads on both sides of the necklace. Trim the excess wire.

5. Run a second strand of stringing wire through the focal bead and the accents on either side of it. Repeat steps 2 and 3, trying to randomize the pearls, vermeil, and any other beads so they are not in exactly the same place as on the first strand. Use clamps to hold both ends before you string them through the final vermeil bead.

6. Repeat step 5 with the third stringing wire, again alternating the pearls and accent beads so they won't align with those on the other two strands.

7. When you have all three strands completed on both sides of the focal bead, loosely braid them together. Remove the clamps. Run the remaining lengths of wire, strands two and three, through the final vermeil bead, through the loop on the clasp and back through the last 1 inch (2.5 cm) of beads and crimps. Use the crimping pliers to crimp the tubes, and the wire cutters to trim any excess wire.

SWEET SPIRAL
HALF-KNOT CHOKER

Spiraling white cord perfectly complements the design on the Venetian glass focal bead. If you're not up on your knots, don't worry. This elegant choker is created using only simple half knots. Tie more knots for a longer necklace or fewer for a shorter one.

WHAT YOU NEED

1 focal bead, 1 to 1½ inches (2.5 to 3.8 cm) long

2 silver ⅝-inch (1.6 cm) silver cones

6 silver 3mm round beads

2 sterling silver 2mm crimp tubes

Sterling silver toggle clasp

Scissors

22 feet (6.7m) of white 1mm synthetic, linen, or silk cord

T-pins

Knotting board

Crimping pliers

Finished length: 16 inches (40.6 cm)

INSTRUCTIONS

Knots used: slip loop knot; overhand knot; half knot

1. Cut two lengths of cord, each 84 inches (2.1 m) long, and four lengths of cord, each 24 inches (61 cm) long.

2. Find the center (halfway) point of the two 84-inch (2.13m) cords and tie them together at that point using a slip-loop knot, as shown in figure 1. Do the same with the four 24-inch (61 cm) cords. Use the T-pins to secure the four cords to your knotting board

through the slip-loop knot, then secure the two-strand tie-up to the board slightly above the four-strand tie-up. Note: Since you're working the piece from the midpoint, your knotting will begin with the six strands that fall below the anchoring points on your knotting board. Be sure to place the six strands that are above out of the way to be worked later.

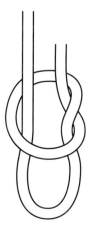

Figure 1

3. Begin the knotting. Tie half knots, as shown in figure 2—two long outside strands around four—until the piece is 1 inch (2.5 cm) long.

4. Remove the slip-loop knots from the cords after loosening them from the board, turn the knotted piece upside down, and secure it to the board using T-pins through the completed half knots.

Figure 2

5. Gather the six ends of cord that fall below the anchored knotting and thread them through your focus bead. Slide the bead into place against the 1 inch (2.5 cm) of knotting. Placing T-pins to either side of the six strands and against the bead will hold it in position.

6. Begin your half knotting on this half of the choker, tying half knots with the long outside strands around the four shorter knot-bearing strands. After you make three or four half knots, the outside knotting strands will start to rotate into their positions. For uniformity in your knotting, after four half knots you should change the positions of the left and right knotting strands in the direction of the spiral, and continue this practice as you work both sides of the piece.

7. Continue tying the half knots until this half of the piece measures 5 inches (12.7 cm). Carefully snip out two of the knot-bearing strands just below the last half knot. Then continue tying half knots for 2 inches (5 cm) more.

8. Turn the piece upside down and repeat step seven.

9. To finish the piece, begin by cutting out the two knot-bearing cords on each end of the choker just below the last half knot. Then tie one overhand knot with the two remaining knotting strands on each end. Make sure to pull the overhand knot snugly against the completed knotting.

10. Cut out one knotting strand on each end approximately ⅛ inch (3mm) below the overhand knot.

11. Thread the cones on each end using the single knotting strands, then thread three silver beads on each cord.

12. Thread the single strand at each end through a silver crimp tube, then loop them through the rings on both sides of the toggle clasp. Carefully pull the strand in place, but leave enough space, or looseness, to allow the toggle to move once the crimp bead is set. Use the crimping pliers to crush the crimps. Then, using fine-point scissors, trim the cord close to the crimp.

DESIGNER: LAURIE SHAW

Handmade glass beads by John Winter of Winterglas

HANDMADE GLASS BEADS AND
RAW EMERALDS

The handmade glass beads possess a rough organic beauty. Combining them with raw emeralds and jaspers gives this design its complex yet harmonious texture. Added to this are touches of shimmering light—courtesy of the perfectly placed silver beads.

WHAT YOU NEED

3 handmade glass beads—1 large elongated tapered tube, two large rounds

2 rectangular artist jaspers

1 faceted round jasper

Black etched glass rondelles

Large raw emerald chips

Variety of hill tribe silver beads

Flexible beading wire*

Silver S-hook

Crimp beads

* *To accommodate the weight of the beads, use beading wire with a thicker diameter.*

Finished length: 38 inches (96.5 cm)

INSTRUCTIONS

1. Using a crimp bead, attach the beading wire to one side of the S-hook.

2. String the beads as desired. Notice how the elongated handmade glass bead is strung to be worn to the side of the necklace. Setting it off-center not only accommodates its shape, it brings the eye right to it. The large silver bead opposite echoes the shape of the glass bead to further highlight it.

3. Once the beads are strung, attach the other side of the S-hook to the beading wire with a crimp bead.

DESIGNER: SUSIE RAGLAND

DRAGONFLY NECKLACE

Rendered in silver, the delicate tracings of dragonfly wings are artfully captured on this large focal bead. The rough-cut amethyst and quartz add to this necklace's texture. Placing the focal bead off-center lets the dragonflies take flight.

WHAT YOU NEED

1 sterling silver dragonfly bead

15 rough-cut amethyst nuggets*

15 green tourmalated quartz rounded beads*

13 sterling silver Bali bead caps

13 sterling silver 3mm faceted rondelles

2 frosted-glass 3mm rondelles

2 sterling silver crimp beads

1 sterling silver toggle

Flexible beading wire

Wire cutters

Crimping pliers

*Amount of beads used will be relative to their size.

Finished length: 22½ inches (57.2 cm)

INSTRUCTIONS

1. Select thicker diameter beading wire to accommodate the weight of the beads. Cut the wire to the
desired length.

2. String on a crimp bead, a silver 3mm rondelle,
and one of the 3mm frosted-glass rondelles. Pass the
wire through the loop on one side of the toggle and
back through the beads and crimp. Use the crimping
pliers to crush the crimp.

3. Start with a green quartz, then a bead cap, an
amethyst, and a silver 3mm rondelle. When you
come to the place you've determined for stringing
the focal bead, string a green quartz, a bead cap,
the focal bead, a bead cap and a green quartz.
Continue stringing in the pattern as before, ending
with a green quartz.

4. String on a crimp bead, a silver rondelle, and the
other glass rondelle. Pass the wire through the loop
on the other side of the toggle, then back down
through the beads and crimp and the green quartz.
Crush the crimp, and trim the excess wire.

RESIN BEAD NECKLACE

Consider this necklace wearable art. Just like minimalist sculpture, the clean, spare lines of the design invite you to comtemplate the quiet serenity of balanced form. The frosted-resin surface on the blue-green beads accents the contemporary feel.

WHAT YOU NEED

2 large resin beads

1 sterling silver cable neck wire

4-inch (10.2 cm) length of 14-gauge sterling silver wire

Small anvil and hammer

Small motorized craft tool with drill bit

Small file

Finished length: neck wire, 16 inches (40.6 cm); dangle, 3½ inches (8.9 cm)

INSTRUCTIONS

1. Place one end of the 14-gauge wire on the anvil. Using the hammer, flatten it until the end fans out.

2. Using a small motorized craft tool and drill bit, drill a hole in the flattened end of the wire. The drill bit needs to make a hole large enough to accommodate the diameter of the neck wire. Using a file, smooth and round the flattened edges.

3. Thread the two large beads onto the wire. As you did in step 1, flatten the other end of the wire until it fans out. Slide the neck wire through the drilled hole to complete your necklace.

CHUNKY RED CORAL

BEAD LOVE

E ven the most luscious beads can languish in your collection waiting for the right visual spice. In this design, it's the chunky red coral that brings the zing. It's resemblance to a chili pepper isn't lost in the design. Notice how it's strung off-center—this bit of creative bead cookery is the unexpected twist that turns up the heat.

WHAT YOU NEED

1 elongated red coral nugget

11 red coral rounds

14 large pewter spacers

2 large, swirly silver Bali beads

2 blue African glass beads, one round, one rectangle

1 dark amber round

1 large turquoise nugget

1 honey amber oval

2 sterling silver crimp beads

2 sterling silver crimp bead covers

1 sterling silver toggle

Flexible beading wire

Wire cutters

Finished length: 20 ½ inches (52 cm)

INSTRUCTIONS

1. Lay the beads in stringing order. Using a crimp bead, attach one end of the beading wire to either the toggle ring or toggle bar. Cover the crimp with a crimp bead cover.

2. Beginning with a large red coral round, then a spacer, string the beads in the order shown. When worn, you want the two large silver beads to be opposite each other. Make sure the large red coral nugget is off-center.

3. Continue stringing until all beads are on the wire. Using a crimp bead, attach the end of the wire to the remaining piece of the toggle clasp. Cover the crimp with a crimp bead cover. Serve and enjoy!

DESIGNER: CONNE GIBSON

Raku leaves by Tia Montague

RAKU LEAVES WITH PEARLS

Mmmmmmmmm...what's more luxurious than multiple interwoven strands of pearls and turquoise? This necklace certainly lives up to its promise. The lovely raku leaves inspired the design and color selection of the beads. If you can't find the exact leaves, you can substitute other motifs in the design.

WHAT YOU NEED

1 strand green turquoise rounds

1 strand yellow pearls

1 strand olive green pearls

Partial strand of tiny copper-colored pearls

1 large and 4 small raku oak leaves, or other motifs

Sterling silver toggle clasp

4 sterling silver bead tips

2 sterling silver 4mm jump rings

3 packages of olive green #2 silk bead cord

Bead board

3 beading needles

Cyanoacrylate glue

Needle-nose pliers

Small, motorized craft tool with a diamond bit, or diamond bead reamer

Finished length: 20 inches (51 cm)

INSTRUCTIONS

1. Using a bead board that has at least four rows and is marked for sizing, lay out the beads in this order starting with the row closest to you: green turquoise beads, yellow pearls, green pearls. Depending on the desired length of the finished necklace, arrange the beads to match the appropriate sizing marks on the board. Don't forget to figure the clasp in the measurement. Add or subtract beads to reach your desired length.

2. For color accent, take away a few of the green turquoise beads and replace them with the tiny copper-colored pearls. Move some of the yellow pearls to the green-pearl row and some of the green pearls to the yellow-pearl row. Exchange beads as desired until the design looks balanced.

NOTE: You will use three needles and three strands of cord to string the beads. Two of the needles are threaded with a single strand each, but you knot both strands together. One needle is threaded with a single strand. This is done to accommodate passing the cord through the bead tips—two strands fit through the hole of a bead tip, three do not. To thread, use the bead cord to thread two needles, each with a single strand. Knot both of their ends that are farthest from the needles together, and secure the knot with glue. Thread the other needle with one strand of cord, knot the end farthest from the needle, and secure the knot with glue.

3. Depending on the desired length of the finished necklace, place the large raku leaf in the center of the row that is farthest from you. Then space the smaller leaves at equal intervals on either side. For longer or shorter necklaces, adjust the spacing of the leaves accordingly. Keep in mind that knots take up space, too. You may want to draw a beading map that shows the measurements and placement of the leaves as they appear on the bead board. As you string and knot (see Knots on page 24), you can check your work to make sure you're on track. You may need to eliminate some of the beads if the necklace starts growing too long.

4. Start by stringing the toggle clasp. Pass the two needles with two strands through a bead tip from the hook end first—the beads will be strung to the curved side of the bead tip. Tie a knot to hold the bead tip, then, using the needle-nose pliers, attach the bead tip to a jump ring, and the jump ring to the toggle side of the clasp. Pass the needle with the single strand through another bead tip, and tie a knot. Attach this bead tip to the same jump ring that is now attached to the toggle end of the clasp. Pass all three needles

through the first turquoise bead, and tie a knot using all three strands of cord. Add another turquoise bead, tie off, then add another. At this point, test to see if the toggle closes easily by passing the toggle bar through the circle. If not, string on more beads until it does close easily.

5. Now pass two needles through a turquoise bead, and tie off. Take the other needle and pass it through a tiny copper-colored bead, then tie off. Use an odd number of beads to continue stringing and knotting between each bead. To make a junction, weave the strands by passing two needles through one bead. This is where the diamond bit or bead reamer may come in handy, since it may be difficult to pass two cords through the holes of the smaller beads. Note: Staggering the juncture of the strands and changing the size of beads that are next to each other will make the necklace lie more comfortably.

6. Continue to knot and weave, measuring as you work in order to correctly place each leaf. When you get to the end, attach the bead tips and jump ring as you did in step 5 to the circle end of the clasp.

GEMSTONES

Whether rough cut or
polished, gemstones hold the
mystery of buried treasure.
Uncovered and transformed,
they enchant the beader and
enhance the wearer.

DESIGNER: MARGARET ASHLEY AMORY

GEMSTONE AND SILVER NECKLACE

f you find yourself overrun with beads that are odds-and-ends from other projects, why not turn them into their own necklace. The designer happened to have gemstones and crystal beads on hand. Stringing them between sections of fine silver beads allows their individual beauty to shine through. The best part about making this type of necklace is that the variety of colors will complement almost any outfit.

Variety of gemstones*, pearls, and crystal beads

Fine silver hill tribe beads in a variety of interesting shapes

4 silver seed beads

Silver crimp beads

Sterling silver toggle clasp

Flexible beading wire

Bead board

Wire cutters

Crimping pliers

*Used here: jade, iolite, rhodochrosite, adventurine, suzalite, chalcedony, carnelian, labradorite, opal, and carnelian.

Finished length: 30 inches (76.2 cm)

INSTRUCTIONS

1. Select beads based on their color, shape, and size in relation to the fine silver beads used. Place the beads on a bead board with the largest in the center. Arrange the remaining beads according to your liking. As shown in this necklace, the gemstones and crystals have 2 inches (5 cm) of silver beads strung on either side.

2. Determine the finished length of your necklace. Add 6 inches (15.2 cm) to that measurement, and use the wire cutters to cut the beading wire to that length.

3. String the center bead first, then alternate stringing sections of beads on one side of the necklace, then the other. This gives you the opportunity to change your mind from your original arrangement as you work, if desired.

4. Finish each end by stringing a silver seed bead, a crimp bead, and another silver seed bead. Loop the wire through the ring at one end of the toggle, then pass the wire back through the silver seed beads and crimp and a few of the larger silver beads. Use the crimping pliers to crush the crimp. Trim any excess wire.

DESIGNER: GEORGIE ANNE JAGGERS
PMC Heart toggle by ZoaArt

HEART NECKLACE

W ho can resist art with heart? The toggle, made of precious metal clay, creates its own focal point, but it's the fanciful beaded dangles that add the whimsy. Full of fun and movement, this is the necklace to wear when you want to tell the world you're feelin' frisky.

WHAT YOU NEED

Assorted types and sizes of beads, as shown, pearls, crystals, gemstones, and glass

13° seed beads

Heart-shaped toggle clasp

Crimp tubes

1 yard (.9 m) of flexible beading wire

2 lengths of chain, each 1½ inches (3.8 cm) long

24-gauge head pins, enough to put four on every link of chain

Wire cutters

Needle-nose pliers

Round-nose pliers

Finished length: 21½ inches (54.5cm)

INSTRUCTIONS

1. Cut a 10-inch (25.4 cm) length of beading wire. String on a crimp tube, 15 seed beads, and the heart side of the toggle clasp. Run the wire back through the crimp tube, leaving approximately a 1-inch (2.5 cm) tail. Use the needle-nose pliers to crush the crimp flat.

2. String on approximately 2½ inches (6.4 cm) of the assorted beads, making sure the first few beads on the wire cover both the main wire and the tail coming from the crimp. After stringing the last bead, string a crimp tube, 15 seed beads, and an end link of one of the 1½-inch (3.8 cm) lengths of chain. Run the wire back through the crimp and the last few beads. Leave the wire tail hanging out to the side. Before crushing the crimp, tug on the tail to make sure everything is tightly strung, crush the crimp, then trim the excess wire.

3. Determine how many beaded dangles you'll need—you want four hanging off each link of chain. On some of the head pins, string a 1-inch (2.5 cm)

section of seed beads only. On the others, string one seed bead and one of the assorted beads of your choice.

4. Working with one head pin at a time, use the needle-nose and round-nose pliers to begin making a wrapped loop. Once you complete the loop, and before you begin wrapping the wire, open the loop and hook the head pin into a link of chain. Close the loop, then complete wrapping the wire tail around the head pin. Using wire cutters, trim any excess wire. Repeat this step until you have attached the number of dangles you need. Then put the chain with dangles into the palm of your hand and squeeze. This will bend the head pins so they don't look stiff.

5. Cut a 14-inch (35.6 cm) length of beading wire. Thread on a crimp tube, 15 seed beads, and the other end link of the chain. Run the wire back through the crimp tube, leaving about a 1-inch (2.5 cm) tail, then crush the crimp. String on one

excess wire. Embellish this section of chain to look like the one you made in steps 3 and 4.

7. Cut a 10-inch (25.4 cm) length of wire. String on a crimp tube,15 seed beads, and the remaining end link of the chain. Run the wire back through the crimp, leaving approximately a 1-inch (2.5 cm) tail. Use needle-nose pliers to crush the crimp. String on approximately 6 inches (15 cm) of beads ending with a crimp tube, 15 seed beads, and the toggle bar side of the clasp. Run the wire back through the crimp tube. Leave the wire tail hanging out to the side. Before crushing the crimp, tug on the tail to make sure everything is tightly strung, crush the crimp, then trim the excess wire.

of the small assorted beads followed by a crimp tube. Push this crimp up toward the first crimp—the small bead will be sandwiched between them—but don't crush it.

6. String on approximately 9 inches (23 cm) of assorted beads, ending with a crimp tube, small bead, crimp tube, 15 seed beads, and an end link of the other length of chain. Run the wire back through the crimp tube, small bead, crimp tube, and last few beads on the wire. Leave the wire tail hanging out to the side. Before crushing the crimp, tug on the tail to make sure everything is tightly strung, crush the crimp, then trim the

PINK-ON-PINK PEARL AND OPAL SET

Since pink opaque stones are rare in the gem world, these opals from Peru offer wonderful design possibilities. Adding small heishi pearls both mirrors and softens the organic texture of the large nuggets.

WHAT YOU NEED

11 pink opal nuggets

30 natural top-drilled pink heishi pearls

20 small silver Bali flower spacers

2 small pink opal nuggets

6 natural top-drilled pink heishi pearls

2 silver 2mm crimp beads

4 silver 3mm beads with large holes

2 jump rings, each 6mm in diameter

Silver S-hook clasp with 2-inch (5 cm) chain extender

8 silver 2½-inch (6.4 cm) head pins

22 inches flexible beading wire

2 lengths of silver chain, each ¾ inch (1.9 cm) long

2 silver French ear wires

Flat-nose pliers

Crimping pliers

Round-nose pliers

Wire cutters

Finished length: necklace, 16 inches (40.6 cm) with a 2-inch (5 cm) extender; earrings, 1½ inches (3.8 cm)

INSTRUCTIONS

Necklace

1. Cut a 22-inch (55.9 cm) length of flexible beading wire, then string on one crimp bead and one 3mm silver bead. Pass the wire through a jump ring, and thread it back through the silver bead and crimp bead, leaving a 1-inch (2.5 cm) tail of wire coming from the crimp.

2. Crush the crimp, and then string on another 3mm silver bead, making sure to cover the stringing wire and wire tail. Placing the two silver beads on

either side of the crimp bead will help prevent the wire from rubbing on the crimp, thus reducing the chance of breakage at the clasp. It's important to use 3mm silver beads with large holes because it's easier to pass two strands of wire through them.

3. String a pink opal nugget, a silver flower spacer, and three top-drilled heishi pearls. Follow with another silver flower spacer and a pink opal nugget. Repeat this pattern using all of the beads. The necklace should begin and end with a pink opal nugget.

4. String a 3mm silver bead, the last crimp bead, and the last 3mm silver bead. Pass the wire through a jump ring, and then back through the silver and crimp beads and one opal nugget. At this point, before crimping, pick up the necklace and allow it to relax in your hands. You want to feel some play in the beads to prevent the necklace from being too stiff. There should be ⅛ to ¼ inch (3 to 5mm) of wire showing between the last pink opal bead and the silver bead. Crush the crimp and trim the excess wire. Attach the clasp to the jump rings.

Earrings

1. String a pink opal onto a head pin. Using the round-nose pliers, make the loop for a wrapped loop, attach one end of a length of chain to it, then use the flat-nose pliers to hold the loop while you wrap the tail around the wire. Trim any excess wire.

2. String three heishi pearls on three separate head pins. Using wrapped loops, attach them where desired on the length of chain. Attach the ear wire to the middle of the length of chain, allowing the chain to drape and the pearls to dangle. Repeat steps 1 and 2 for the other earring.

TURQUOISE BEAD CHOKER

This elegant design has a playful side. What makes it so much fun is the way your eyes move rhythmically over the beads. While it looks fresh and spontaneous, the layout of the dangles has been carefully choreographed to make sure the beads remain the principal dancers.

BEAD LOVE

WHAT YOU NEED

11 turquoise 12mm beads

11 sterling silver head pins

43 4 x 3mm tube crimp beads

Sterling silver hard neck wire

Wire cutters

Round-nose pliers

Finished length: neck wire, 16 inches (40.6 cm); dangles, 1 to 2½ inches (2.5 to 6.4 cm)

INSTRUCTIONS

1. Trim the head pins to varying lengths from 1 to 4 inches (2.5 to 10.3 cm) long. String a 12mm bead on each head pin, followed by one tube crimp bead.

2. Arrange the beaded dangles in their stringing order, making sure that no beads touch. You want the pattern to look random. When you're satisfied with the layout, snip off any extra length from the head pins as needed.

3. Make a loop on the end of each head pin. To prevent the dangle from falling off the neck wire, make sure each loop is a complete closed circle.

4. String one crimp bead on the neck wire, followed by one dangle, followed by three more crimp beads. Continue alternating one dangle with three crimp beads until the last dangle is on the wire. Then string on one more crimp bead to complete the necklace.

YELLOW OPAL NECKLACE

Here's a beautiful example of a symmetrical design in a monochromatic color scheme. The yellow opals are lustrous and luminescent. Discovered in Africa a few years ago by miners digging for diamonds, the yellow opal offers beaders the option of rich color and texture. Classified as a jelly opal, it exhibits the clear, glowing shade common to that family of gemstones.

WHAT YOU NEED

21 large, tumbled, yellow opal beads

12 faceted yellow opal barrels

8 6mm yellow opal rondelles

6 silver 3mm beads with large holes

4 silver 2mm crimp beads

8 sterling silver Bali bead caps

2 sterling silver 6 mm jump rings

Sterling silver S-hook clasp with 2-inch (5 cm) extender chain

Wire cutters

28 inches (71 cm) of .018 (.457mm) diameter flexible beading wire

Crimping pliers

Finished length: 20 inches (50.8 cm) with 2-inch (5 cm) extender chain

INSTRUCTIONS

1. Cut a 28-inch (71 cm) length of flexible beading wire, then string on one crimp bead, one 3mm silver bead, another crimp bead, and another 3mm bead. Pass the wire through a jump ring, and thread it back through the beads and crimps, leaving a 1-inch (2.5 cm) tail of wire coming from the last crimp. Use the crimping pliers to crush the crimps. Note: Use two crimps for extra security when stringing heavy stones.

2. String on another 3mm silver bead, making sure you cover the stringing wire and tail left from step 1, then string on a silver Bali bead cap. Alternate stringing faceted barrels with rondelles, ending with a barrel, until three barrels have been strung. String on a bead cap.

3. String seven of the tumbled yellow opal beads. Repeat stringing a series of barrels and rondelles followed by a series of tumbled stones, until you have four groupings of barrels and rondelles with Bali bead caps, and three groupings of tumbled stones. String on a 3mm silver bead.

4. String on a crimp, a 3mm silver bead, another crimp, and another 3mm bead. Pass the wire through a jump ring, and then back through the silver and crimp beads and the first barrel bead. At this point, before crimping, pick up the necklace and allow it to relax in your hands. You want to feel some play in the beads to prevent the necklace from being too stiff. There should be 1/8 to 1/4 inch (3 to 6mm) of wire showing between the Bali bead cap and the first 3mm silver bead. Crush the crimps and trim the excess wire. Attach the clasp to the jump rings.

TAKE-FIVE FACETED TURQUOISE NECKLACE

L arge faceted gemstones—the divas of the bead world—love to take center stage. The trick is finding a compatible stringing design that matches their dramatic scale. For this bold necklace, doubling the chain seems to beautifully solve the problem. In fact, you could say it's the strong supporting cast that quietly holds the plot together.

5 large faceted turquoise beads

30 inches (76 cm) of sterling silver 3.9mm rolo chain

11 sterling silver 4mm 16-gauge jump rings

12 inches (30.5 cm) of 20-gauge sterling silver wire

Toggle clasp

Round-nose pliers

Needle-nose pliers

Wire cutters

Liver of sulphur

0000 steel wool

Finished length: 22½ inches (57 cm)

INSTRUCTIONS

1. Oxidize the silver chain, toggle clasp, and jump rings for an antiqued look. Dissolve the liver of sulphur in hot water. Add the silver pieces, remove them, and dry thoroughly. Use 0000 steel wool to rub off the dark finish and polish the silver.

2. Using wire cutters, cut the rolo chain into eight 2-inch (5 cm) lengths, and four 3½-inch (8.9 cm) lengths.

3. Cut the sterling silver wire into five 2-inch (5 cm) lengths. Thread each bead onto a length of wire. Using the round-nose pliers, wrap the end of the wire twice to make double loops on both ends of the bead.

4. Attach a jump ring to each loop. Then attach two 2-inch (5 cm) lengths of chain to one end of each bead. Connect the five beads by attaching the double chains to the jump rings on the beads.

5. Attach two 3½-inch (8.9 cm) lengths of rolo chain to each of the remaining jump rings on the end of the string of beads. Using jump rings, attach the ends of the chains to the toggle clasp.

FLUORITE AND PINK PEARL
RIBBON NECKLACE

M ixing cool pink pearls with small rough-cut fluorite beads may seem like a strange combination, but in this necklace it's pure romance—then there's the ribbon! This flirty pairing of textures seems to evoke parasols, sundresses, and long weekends in the country.

WHAT YOU NEED

35 fluorite beads, approximately ¼ to ½ inch (6 to 13mm) in size

18 pink pearls, approximately 5mm in size

53 sterling silver head pins

4 inches (10.2 cm) of sterling silver 5 to 6mm oval chain

¾-inch-wide (1.9 cm) pink ribbon

Round-nose pliers

Wire cutters

Chain-nose pliers

Scissors

Finished length: beading, 4 inches (10.2 cm)

INSTRUCTIONS

1. Thread the fluorite beads and pink pearls onto the head pins.

2. Using your round-nose pliers, make a loop at the end of each head pin, leaving enough of a tail to wrap. Wrap the wire tail around the head pin until its end rests against the last bead. Use the wire cutters to trim any excess as needed. (See Making a Wrapped Loop on page 25.)

3. Using the chain-nose pliers to open the links of the chain, attach each head pin by its loop to the chain. Make sure you evenly space the pearl and fluorite bead dangles for a good color mix.

4. Using the scissors, cut two lengths of pink ribbon, each approximately 5 feet (1.5 m) long. Thread one end of each ribbon through the last link on each side of the silver chain and double the ribbons.

5. Using a simple overhand knot, knot each doubled ribbon approximately 6 inches (15.2 cm) from each end of the chain. You can trim the ribbons as desired, or leave them long and flowing.

SIMPLY GEM EARRINGS

W hile purchased ear wires are certainly convenient to use, sometimes you need a little extra. You may find that a special bead or combination of beads calls for a custom treatment. These three lovely examples use the same technique for making ear wires to accommodate the beads used in the designs.

Beads as shown: large polished raw emerald chips, amber hex rondelles, silver Bali beads, large emerald hex rondelles

20-gauge sterling silver wire

Wire cutters

Needle-nose pliers

Burnishing tool

Small anvil

Ring mandrel or ¾-inch (1.9 cm) dowel

File

Round-nose pliers

Finished length: 1 to 1¼ inches (2.5 to 3.2 cm)

INSTRUCTIONS

1. Cut the wire. You'll need approximately 3 inches (7.6 cm) of wire for each earring.

2. Thread the wire through the bead or beads. Using the needle-nose pliers, make a loop (see Making a Simple Loop on page 24). Do not close the loop all the way. You want it slightly open to accommodate the wire that will come from the other side to close the earring.

3. Bend the ear wire on the other side of the bead or beads straight up. Work harden the wire by laying it on the anvil and rubbing it with the burnishing tool. This will help the wire keep its arc once you shape it.

4. Shape the arc of the wire by laying the wire on top of the mandrel or dowel and smoothing it around the curve of the tool.

5. Allow approximately ¼ inch (6mm) of wire to extend from the loop when the earring is closed. Trim the wire as needed, and use the file to smooth the end. Using round-nose pliers, put a slight upward curve at the end of the wire.

BIRTHSTONES

Many different cultures believe semiprecious and precious gemstones can be portents of good fortune. Knowing the stones assigned to each birth month can help you when giving or receiving.

January, garnet

February, amethyst

March, aquamarine

April, diamond

May, emerald

June, pearl

July, ruby

August, peridot

September, sapphire

October, opal

November, citrine

December, blue topaz

SPRING BOUQUET EARRINGS

A riot of soft color offsets the pastel faceted briolettes, creating the unmistakable look of spring. More beads are added at the bottom of the chain drops to balance the design. This not only imparts movement to the earrings, but gives them the appearance of flowers spilling from a garden basket.

WHAT YOU NEED

2 faceted 16 x 25mm gemstone briolette drops

16 faceted 4mm glass beads in various colors

12 vintage glass flower beads, 4 each in purple, pink, and blue

4 vintage wired glass leaves

5 inches (12.7 cm) of 22-gauge dead soft, round, gold-filled wire

1½ inches (4 cm) of gold-filled 2mm chain

40 gold-filled head pins

4 rhinestone head pins

Gold-filled lever-back ear wires

Needle-nose pliers

Round-nose pliers

Wire cutters

Finished length: 2½ inches (6.4 cm)

INSTRUCTIONS

1. Cut the 22-gauge wire in half to make two, 2½-inch (6.4 cm) lengths. Then cut the chain in half to make two ¾-inch (1.9 cm) lengths. Slip a briolette onto one of the lengths of wire. On one side of the bead, leave a 1-inch (2.5 cm) tail.

2. Using the needle-nose pliers, wrap the shorter end around the longer tail a few times, trimming any excess. Now use your round-nose pliers to form a small wrapped loop from the remaining wire tail, but before you wrap the wire to close the loop, attach it to an end link on one of the lengths of chain. Close the loop, complete wrapping the wire, and trim any excess.

3. String the 4mm glass beads on the gold-filled and rhinestone head pins. String the vintage flower beads on the gold-filled head pins only. Use the needle-nose and round-nose pliers to make wrapped loops at the end of each head pin for attaching the beads to the chain (see Making a Wrapped Loop on page 25). Begin attaching the beads to the links closet to the briolette and work your way up the chain.

4. Attach the wired leaves, two per earring, close to the briolette. Add more beads to the bottom of the chain, gradually adding less as you get to the top. Randomly place two of the rhinestone head pins with beads on each earring.

5. Repeat the steps to make the second earring, then attach the lever-back ear wires to each.

ROUGH RUBY NUGGETS SUITE

BEAD LOVE

The designer shares that he "fell in lust" with a strand of rough ruby nugget beads. He loved their soft color, oddly shaped facets, and matte surfaces. Though it took him a bit of time and effort to find beads that would complement the shape of the nuggets, a little online sleuthing finally did the trick.

WHAT YOU NEED

Rough ruby nugget beads

Faceted Thai silver beads

Electroformed sterling silver beads

Sterling silver crimp beads

Sterling silver head pins

1 sterling silver two-strand box clasp

1 pair silver ball post earrings with ring

Flexible beading wire

Wire cutters

Crimping pliers

Round-nose pliers

Needle-nose pliers

Abrasive scrub pads

*Finished length: bracelet, 8 inches (20.5 cm);
earrings, 1¾ inches (4.4 cm)*

INSTRUCTIONS

Bracelet

1. As purchased, the electroformed beads and box clasp chosen for this bracelet had a high-polish finish that looked jarring against the matte finish of the nuggets. The designer used an abrasive scrubbing pad on the beads and box clasp to matte the shiny finish.

2. Cut two lengths of beading wire longer than the actual length you desire your bracelet to be.

3. Loop one length around one of the box clasp loops. Thread a crimp bead on the two ends of the wire you just looped. Snug a crimp bead up against the loop, and use the crimping pliers to crimp the bead in place. Repeat with the second length of bead wire.

4. Alternate sterling silver beads and nuggets along each strand of wire. When you are satisfied with the positioning of each strand, thread a crimp bead on the end of each wire. Working with one wire at a time, loop the wire around one of the clasp loops, thread it back through the crimp bead, and tighten the wire loop against the clasp. Use crimping pliers to crimp the bead. Repeat with the second wire.

5. Trim the wires as needed.

Earrings

1. Thread the nuggets and sterling silver beads onto a head pin.

2. Using round-nose pliers, make a wrapped loop at one end of the wire.

3. Using the needle-nose pliers, open the ring of the ball-post earrings, slip the wrapped loop onto the ring, and then close the ring.

4. Make a second earring following the previous steps. Take care that the second earring is the same length as the first.

GREEN TURQUOISE
SPIKES COLLAR

BEAD LOVE

W e think you get the point—this is one great necklace. It's delicate yet edgy, interesting, and fun. The colors would brighten basic black, but the design would pair well with a sundress and sandals. Add the long dangle earrings if you dare.

WHAT YOU NEED

Green turquoise spikes in graduated lengths

Silver head pins, extra-long

3mm garnet rounds

8mm turquoise rounds

4mm garnet rounds

Silver Bali heishi spacers

Garnet seed beads

Crimp tubes

Silver toggle clasp

Ear wires

Flexible beading wire

Wire cutters

Round-nose pliers

Finished length: necklace, 20 inches (50.8 cm);
earrings, 3 inches (7.6 cm)

INSTRUCTIONS

Necklace

1. Lay out the spikes in the order you prefer. You may want to string them in a random pattern, as shown, or may prefer a more graduated look.

2. Next, string a head pin with a 3mm garnet, an 8mm turquoise round, and another 3mm garnet. If you're making a necklace with a random pattern, use the wire cutters to trim the head pins to different lengths. For a graduated pattern, trim each head pin to be slightly shorter than the spike next to it. Use the round-nose pliers to make a small wrapped loop at the top of each head pin.

3. On a length of flexible beading wire, string a spike, then a 3mm garnet, a head pin with beads, and a 3mm garnet. Repeat this sequence 10 to 12 times, ending with a spike. Center this grouping of beads on the beading wire.

4. On one side, string an 8mm turquoise round. Then string a spacer, a 4mm garnet, a spacer, and five 8mm turquoise rounds, repeating this sequence until you reach the desired length. Repeat this pattern on the other side.

5. To finish, string three 4mm garnets and a crimp tube on the end. Loop the wire through the ring on one side of the toggle clasp, then take the wire back through the crimp and several beads. Use the crimping pliers to crush the crimp. Trim any excess wire. Repeat on the other side.

Earrings

1. Thread a spike on an extra-long head pin. Cut off the stop. Using the round-nose pliers, make a wrapped loop for attaching the spike to the ear wire.

2. Cut the stop off a head pin and string on three garnet seed beads, an 8mm turquoise round, and three more seed beads. Make wrapped loops on both ends of the wire, and attach them to the wire sides of the wrapped loop you made for the spike.

3. Thread three 4mm garnet beads on three separate head pins. Make wrapped loops on the ends of each. Attach them to the wrapped loop at the top of the spike. Repeat for the other earring.

LAND AND SEA

Shaped to perfection or left in their organic form, gifts from earth and sea provide beads for endless designs. Pearls, wood, bone, amber—who can ask for more?

MABE PEARLS
NECKLACE AND EARRINGS

If the luster of pearls is your look of choice, the unusual shape of mabe pearls gives you even more to love. The flat back and rounded top of these cultured pearls resemble a cabochon. The versatile length of this necklace allows the wearer to double it, wear the clasp at the back or side, or layer the piece with other jewelry. Strung with fine silver tube beads and a vintage box clasp, the look is sheer elegance.

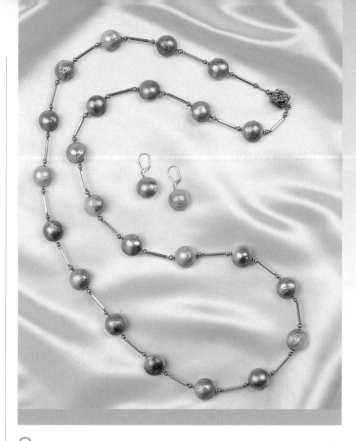

WHAT YOU NEED

Mabe pearls

2mm freshwater pearls

Fine silver faceted seed beads

Silver crimp beads

Fine silver hill tribe tube beads

Vintage silver clasp

Flexible beading wire

Silver ear wires

Crimping pliers

Silver head pins

Bead board

Wire cutters

Round-nose pliers

Finished length: necklace, 40 inches (101.6 cm); earrings, ¾ inch (1.9 cm)

INSTRUCTIONS

Necklace

1. Lay the beads on a bead board, then use the wire cutters to cut an appropriate length of flexible beading wire. Use thicker diameter beading wire to accommodate the weight of the beads.

2. String a 2mm pearl, a seed bead, a crimp bead, and a seed bead. Loop the wire through the ring on one end of the box clasp and pass the wire back through the beads, pearl, and crimp bead. Use the crimping pliers to crush the crimp. Trim any excess wire.

3. Follow an alternating sequence of seed bead, tube bead, seed bead, 2mm pearl, seed bead, mabe, until you reach the desired length for the necklace.

4. Finish the strand with a 2mm pearl, seed bead, crimp bead, and seed bead. Loop the wire through the ring on the other side of the box clasp, and pass the wire back through the beads, pearl, and crimp bead. Use the crimping pliers to crush the crimp. Trim any excess wire.

Earrings

1. String a single mabe pearl on a head pin.

2. Use the round-nose pliers to make a wrapped loop for attaching the head pin to the ear wire. Repeat for the other earring.

NATURAL EXPRESSIONS
BRACELET

Seeds, horn, wood—wearing big beads made of natural materials is HOT. Using satin ribbon as the stringing material brings an unexpected touch of coyness to the bold design—the fringy knots acting as an inviting wink. The large beads are each approximately 20mm in diameter.

WHAT YOU NEED

3 round solid-wood beads

2 tiger-pattern kukui nut beads

2 large round horn beads

2 coco shell disc spacers

2 7mm carved latticework wooden beads

3½ feet (1.1m) of ⅜-inch (9.5mm) wide ribbon

Big-eyed beading needle

Sharp scissors

Finished length: 8 inches (20.3 cm)

INSTRUCTIONS

1. Thread the ribbon on the needle, then slide each bead onto the ribbon. Start and end with a latticework bead. Randomly string on the spacers.

2. Use sharp scissors to cut four approximately 4-inch (10.2 cm) lengths from the longest end of the ribbon. Center the beads on the remaining length.

3. Using a simple overhand knot, tie each short piece of ribbon to the stringing ribbon between the large beads. Do not tie knots between beads where you've strung spacers. To finish, cut the ends of the knotted ribbon on the diagonal.

4. When all beads have been added, position them so there is an equal length of ribbon on either side, then make knots on the sides of the end beads. Tie a bow, and go.

ALEURITES MOLUCCANA

Kukui nuts, also called candlenuts, come from the South Seas—the candlenut tree is the state tree of Hawaii. Polynesians would make torches from these oil-rich kernels by impaling them on sticks before lighting them. Dark blue dye made from charred candlenuts is used as ink for tattoos. Though rather unremarkable in their raw state, they make beautiful beads when polished.

WITH-A-TWIST SHELL NECKLACE

BEAD LOVE

Can you fall in love with a finding? Sometimes you can't help yourself. The box clasp, with its detachable screen top, makes it possible to add the lush mound of beaded loops to this design. Plus, the clasp accommodates three strands of beads.

WHAT YOU NEED

Dark green dyed-shell points

Light green dyed-shell points

6mm jade rounds

7mm faceted synthetic quartz rounds

11° seed beads in assorted colors

8° seed beads in assorted colors

6° seed beads in assorted colors

12 copper crimp tubes

14° seed beads in assorted colors

2 yards (1.8m) of flexible beading wire

3-strand box clasp with detachable screen

Size D dark brown beading thread

Size 12 beading needle

Wire cutters

Needle-nose pliers

Scissors

Finished length: 17 inches (43.2 cm)

INSTRUCTIONS

1. Cut the flexible beading wire approximately 8 inches (20.3 cm) longer than the desired finished length of the necklace.* Thread on a crimp tube, seven 14° seed beads, one of the small rings on one side of the clasp, and seven more 14° seed beads. Run the wire back through the crimp tube, leaving a tail approximately 1 inch (2.5 cm) long. Make sure the beads that form the loop around the ring of the clasp are snug, then use the needle-nose pliers to crush the crimp.

2. Thread on one 8° seed bead followed by a crimp tube, making sure they cover the wire tail left in step 1. Use the needle-nose pliers to flatten the crimp. String the dark green points on the strand, ending with a crimp tube, an 8° seed bead, another crimp tube, seven 14° seed beads, the matching ring on the opposite end of the clasp, and seven more 14° seed beads. Run the wire down through the crimp tube, the 8° seed bead, the other crimp tube, and a few beads on the strand. Use your pli-

ers to tighten the wire so the beads snug up against each before crushing both crimps. Use the wire cutters to trim away the excess wire.

3. Repeat steps 1 and 2 for each of the other strands. String one strand with light green points and the other with alternating jade and synthetic quartz.

4. Remove the screen from the box clasp. Cut a 2-yard (1.8m) length of beading thread, then thread it on the needle, doubling the thread. For an anchor bead, tie several knots around as 11° seed bead.

5. Coming from underneath the screen, push the needle through one of the center holes. Thread on alternating small 6° and large 11° seed beads. When you have a length of strung beads that will make a loop the size you desire, take the needle back through the same hole. From underneath the screen, move the needle to a hole beside the first, and repeat the process using different seed beads. Continue making loops as you work out from the center to the edges of the screen.

6. When the screen is completely covered with beaded loops, tie off the thread using the same method of knotting you did for the anchor bead in step 4. Replace the screen on the clasp, using the needle-nose pliers to fold the prongs on the clasp over the screen to secure it.

* When worn, twist the strands slightly before closing the clasp. The extra length of wire you add before cutting it compensates for the length lost in the twisting.

PRIMITIVE PEARL NECKLACE

Though this necklace uses materials that were accessible to cultures centuries ago, it couldn't be more contemporary. To give this necklace its look of fashionable, aged comfort, the designer used groupings of glass beads in muted subtle tones. To close the necklace, a sliding bead recreates what must have been a distant ancestor of today's toggle.

WHAT YOU NEED

Large, round mother-of-pearl pendant

1 large wooden 16mm bead with large hole

3 wooden 8mm beads with large holes

Assorted glass, shell, and wooden beads with large holes

Various metal spacers

Leather cord

Bead board

Scissors

Finished length: 23 inches (58.4 cm)

INSTRUCTIONS

1. Cut three pieces of leather cord, each approximately 36 inches (91.4 cm) long. Take one length of cord, and fold it in half. Thread the loop made by folding it through the back of the pendant. Thread the two ends of the cord though the loop. Take the other two lengths of cord and thread them horizontally through the loop, centering them to have two equal lengths on either side of the pendant. Pull the two ends of the first cord to tighten the loop.

2. On each side of the necklace, string all three strands of cord through an 8mm wooden bead. Push the wooden bead close to the pendant.

3. Using three rows on the bead board (if you don't have one, you can place the beads on a towel so they don't roll away), lay out the beads and spacers, placing them where you want them on the necklace.

4. Working with one row of beads at a time, and starting with one strand of cord on one side of the necklace, use the marks on the bead board to measure the distance from the pendant to the first group of beads. String on the beads, positioning them at the point you measured, and make an overhand knot on either side of the beads to secure them. Continue measuring and stringing beads on both sides of the pendant until that row on the bead board is strung.

5. Repeat step 4 on the remaining two strands until you've strung all the beads.

6. On one side of the necklace, approximately 2 inches (5 cm) from the end of the strands, make a knot using all three strands. String on the 16mm bead, and make another knot using all three strands to secure it.

7. On the other side of the necklace, string all three strands of cord through one 8mm wooden bead. Make a knot at least 2 inches (5 cm) from the last set of beads, so the large bead on the other end of the necklace can pass through the strands.

8. To fasten the necklace, slide the 8mm wooden bead down the strands, and slip the large wooden bead through the loops of cord. To secure the closure, push the smaller wood bead up towards the larger bead. Cut off any excess cord.

DESIGNER: NANCY KUGEL

CICADA LARIAT

The large, carved netsuke cicada bead reminded the designer of her childhood summers spent with her grandmother. When they visited the nearby botanic gardens, they would find cast-off cicadas shells. Her grandmother showed her how to place it on her blouse like a brooch, and they would wear their matching jewelry with pride. Netsuke and ojime, such as those used in this necklace, make great focal beads.

WHAT YOU NEED

4 hand-carved ojime

1 hand-carved netsuke

Assortment of unique and earthy beads

11° seed beads

Black onyx ring, 1¼ inches (3.2 cm) in diameter

4mm crystal or glass beads

2 lengths of flexible beading wire, each 35 inches (89 cm) long

Crimp beads

Crimping pliers

Wire cutters

Finished length: 31 inches (78.7 cm)

INSTRUCTIONS

1. Working with one strand of flexible beading wire, string a length of 11° seed beads long enough to make a beaded loop when passed through the onyx ring.

2. Pass the second strand of beading wire through the seed beads and center the beads on the strands. Pass both strands through the onyx ring, doubling them to make four strands. The ring should fit snuggly in the beaded loop made in step 1. If needed, adjust the fit of the loop by adding or removing seed beads.

3. String one 4mm crystal or bead, then a crimp bead on all four strands together. Snug the bead and crimp tight to the ring before using the crimping pliers to crush the crimp. Slide all four strands through the netsuke, then string another 4mm crystal or bead on all four strands together.

4. String the assortment of beads on each of the four strands. Mix them up any way you like to create your own bead soup. End each strand with an ojime and, for extra security, two crimps. Crush the crimps. Trim any excess wire.

NETSUKE AND OJIME

The large cicada bead used in this project is an example of the ancient Japanese art form called *netsuke*. Japanese artists created these intricate carvings to serve as a means for attaching carved boxes known as *inro*, that were used for carrying essentials, to their kimonos. A cord that was passed through the holes in the *netsuke* enabled the box to hang from the kimono's sash. The *inro* itself was held shut by small *ojime* beads, like the ones used in the project to finish the ends of the lariat.

NEPALESE
AMBER AND TEKTITE

A jacket made from African mudcloth inspired the designer to make this necklace. It seems only natural that fabric painted with dyes made from mineral-rich mud would connect the mind to earthy amber and tektite. You can't see them, but in order to keep the pendant from becoming "jiggly," four small E beads (larger seed beads in sizes 4°, 5°, or 6°) hide under its generous bail.

WHAT YOU NEED

1 vintage Nepalese amber and silver bead

30 large, flat tektite or black stone chips similar in size to the amber*

60 small sterling silver flat-flower Bali spacers

30 large flat amber chips of similar size*

2 small flat amber chips

8 black E beads

2 sterling silver crimp beads

1 silver toggle

Flexible beading wire**

Crimping pliers

Wire cutters

*The number of beads you use will depend on their size and the length of the finished necklace.

**To accommodate the weight of the beads, use wire with a thicker diameter.

Finished length: 20 inches (50.8 cm)

INSTRUCTIONS

1. Lay the beads in stringing order. To attach the toggle, string an E bead and crimp bead onto the beading wire. Pass the wire through the toggle connector, back through the E bead, and into the crimp.

2. String on another E bead, then string the beads in order of tektite, Bali spacer, amber, and Bali spacer. Continue stringing in this way until you reach the center of the necklace. End the last series with tektite, Bali spacer, and one of the small amber chips.

3. String on four E beads, then the pendant, which will go right over the four small beads. Reverse the stringing order to complete the other half of the necklace.

BIG AND BEAUTIFUL
WOODEN BEADS

BEAD LOVE

ncredibly lush wooden beads speak for themselves. Spacing them on waxed cord shows off each beautiful grain pattern. Keep in mind that heavier beads need a thicker thread to support them. To complement the scale and weight of the beads used, the designer twisted six strands of cord together and worked them as one.

WHAT YOU NEED

Wooden beads with 4 to 5mm holes*

5-ply #18 waxed-linen cord in brown and black

Scissors

Needle

Size A waxed bead thread

Beading tweezers, optional

Bead board or soft cloth

Finished length: 42 inches (106.5 cm)

Wooden beads used here: Australian grass tree; jarrah burl; blackbutt burl; ancient red gum; mulga; Tasmanian tiger myrtle; white top burl; brown mallee burl; orange conkerberry; she oak and she-oak nuts; African ebony; wenge; padauk; and Amazonian snakewood.

INSTRUCTIONS

1. Lay your beads out on a bead board or cloth to decide how many beads to use and the order in which you will string them. Determine whether the beads will touch, or will have spacing and knots between each bead or between groupings of beads. Consider the finished length of the necklace and whether you will use a clasp or make a continuous strand.

2. Arrange the beads until you are happy with the result. You can temporarily thread them onto a piece of cord to keep them in order while you test the necklace around your neck for weight and comfort.

3. To determine the length of cord you'll need, first decide on the finished length you want for the necklace. Add 1 inch (2.5 cm) for each knot between beads or groupings of beads. If you're making a continuous strand necklace, add another 12 inches (30.5 cm) to the length, which will be worked as the overlap of 6 inches (15.2 cm) at either end. For example, since this project has a finished length of 42 inches (106.5 cm) and uses 21 beads with two knots between each, an additional 42 inches (106.5 cm) was added for the knots. And, since it's a continuous necklace, an additional 12

inches (30.5 cm) was added, making a total of 96 inches (2.4m) of cord needed for the project.

4. You will use six strands of cord twisted together to work as one. Make sure the thread will pass through all your bead holes. Test to see if a single knot will hold your beads in place without the holes slipping over the knots. You may need to tie a double knot or loop the cord end through the knot an extra one or two times to make a larger knot. Allow extra cord in your calculation for these thicker knots. Cut your cord to length.

5. For this continuous necklace, choose the bead with the largest hole to be the last bead you thread, since it will need to pass through three thicknesses of cord when you overlap to secure and hide the ends. If you can't find one with a larger hole, try drilling out the hole using a larger diameter drill bit or by using a round file inside the hole to make it larger.

6. Tie your first knot 6 inches (15.2 cm) from the end of the cord. Thread on your first bead. Tie a second knot. If needed, tie a double or triple knot to prevent the bead from slipping over the knot.

7. Leave a 1-inch (2.5 cm) length of cord, then tie a third knot, string on the next bead, and knot. Repeat in this way, stringing and knotting, until you have one bead left to string.

8. Trim both ends of the cord to 6 inches (15.2 cm) each. Thread your last bead on one end of your cord, pushing it up against the last knot. Thread the end of that cord back through the last bead, but don't pull all the way through, leaving a small loop showing. Thread the other end of your cord through this loop, folding it back on itself as you do. Pull the end of the first cord until the joining of the cords is hidden inside your bead and you have an even amount of cord left on each side. Knot each loose end against this last bead.

9. Trim the ends of the cord to 1 inch (2.5 cm) or less. Using the needle and fine beading thread, bind and stitch each end to prevent fraying, then push the cord back inside the bead—beading tweezers can help. Using the needle and thread, secure the knots on either side of the bead by taking a few stitches in each.

GLASS, PLASTIC, AND MORE

Beads made from glass,
plastic, and more let
you take your
imagination to
the limits and beyond.
Fun and fantasy come
together when you explore
this realm.

DESIGNER: CHRIS FRANCHETTI

SEEING DOUBLE
VINTAGE NECKLACE

Combining vintage beads and findings from a past aesthetic to create a design that reflects today's trends is both challenging and satisfying. Made almost exclusively of found components, this necklace is truly one of a kind. Although you won't be creating an exact duplicate, look for beads that resemble the ones used here. This will give you an opportunity to indulge in a bead lover's favorite pastime—the thrill of the hunt.

WHAT YOU NEED

5 green vintage pressed-glass tablet beads with floral motif

4 opaque, light green vintage faceted-glass rounds

5 green fire-polished faceted-glass beads

5 dark topaz fire-polished faceted-glass beads

6 brown leopard-swirl glass rondelles

1 jade green vintage molded-glass Buddha bead

13 amber-color vintage glass beads in long, rounded-side tablets

5 citrus-colored Mexican lampworked glass beads in organic shapes

3 brass hourglass tubes

1 antique-brass finish bulldog charm

Vintage brass filigree-bead chain

Ornate brass-plated pewter toggle

20-gauge round brass wire

Bead board

Wire cutters

Round-nose pliers

Smooth-jaw chain-nose pliers

Flat-nose pliers

Chasing hammer and jeweler's block

Finished length: 34 inches (86.4 cm) with a 6-inch (15 cm) fringe

INSTRUCTIONS

1. Choose a mix of bead colors, shapes, and textures, then lay them on a bead board. Select beads that will go together to make linked groupings. For example, in this necklace three amber-color tablet beads make one grouping; an opaque green faceted-glass round, a small green faceted-glass bead, and a medium brown, leopard swirl rondelle make another; and so on.

2. Cut lengths of wire that are long enough to make wrapped loops on either side of each bead. Working

3. Divide the chain you're using into varying lengths. The purchased vintage chain is made from a series of small filigree balls strung on wire connected by simple loops. The loops were unsoldered, making it easy to divide the chain using chain-nose pliers.

4. Link the bead groupings to the chain lengths as desired. Since the design is a double necklace—a choker within a longer rope length—you'll make the choker and the two sides separately before attaching them. Make two equal lengths, each approximately 17 inches (43.2 cm) long, and one shorter length for the choker approximately 15 inches (38.1 cm) long. It's important that each length begins and ends with chain.

5. Make four short bead-and-chain lengths for the tassels. Vary the lengths for more interest. Include the bulldog charm on one of the lengths.

6. Use the round-nose pliers and wire to make two double-wrapped loops. Attach the loops, each to an end of one of the longer lengths, then attach the choker to the same loops. Next, attach the bar side of the toggle to one of the double loops, and the ring side to the other.

7. Join the necklace and attach the tassels with a simple figure-eight loop. To make it, use the widest part of the round-nose pliers to make one large loop in a length of wire. Wrap the tail around the base of the loop a few times. Then make another loop from the tail on the other side of the wrapping (at this point, it will look like a figure eight). To finish, wrap the remaining tail at the base of the second loop around the first wrapping. Attach the ends of the necklace to one loop and the beaded tassels to the other.

8. A flattened coil adds a finishing touch to the end of each tassel. To make one, use the round-nose pliers to make a tiny loop at the end a length of wire, then use the flat-nose pliers to coil wire around the loop a few times. Lay the coil on the jeweler's block and use a chasing hammer to flatten it. String a bead on the wire, make a wrapped loop, and attach it to the end of the tassel. Repeat for the other tassels.

in bead groupings, string each bead in the group on a length of wire, then use the round-nose pliers to make wrapped loops (see Making a Wrapped Loop on page 25) for attaching the beads together as you work.

DESIGNER: RAIN NEWCOMB

MOTHER-OF-PEARL
LARIAT NECKLACE

A simple weaving stitch, odd-count tubular peyote to be exact, creates the lovely rope for this lariat. Before you know it, a circle of nine seed beads will grow to great lengths. When weaving, try using a thread color that matches the accent beads rather than the seed beads. The orange thread used here creates a subtle visual line that carries your eye right to the mother-of-pearl dangles.

WHAT YOU NEED

4 mother-of-pearl squares

1 tube 11° green seed beads

4 head pins

Size 12 beading needle

Beading thread

Round-nose pliers

Wire cutters

Finished length: 34 inches (86.4 cm)

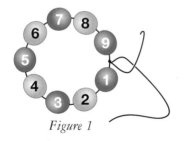

Figure 1

INSTRUCTIONS

1. Thread the needle with approximately 1 yard (.9 m) of beading thread. Thread on nine seed beads. Make a circle by knotting the thread, as shown in figure 1, leaving a 4-inch (10.2 cm) tail that you'll weave back in later.

2. Pass the needle back through the first bead you threaded. Pick up one seed bead and go through the next bead in the circle, as shown in figure 2. Continue to add one bead at a time until you've completed the circle.

3. Go around the circle again, adding a seed bead in between each of the beads you added in step 2, as shown in figure 3. If you want to keep the tiny beads from rolling around too much as you work, place them on a dinner plate covered with a cloth napkin.

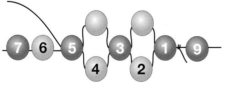

Figure 2

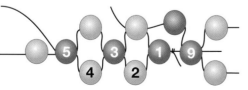

Figure 3

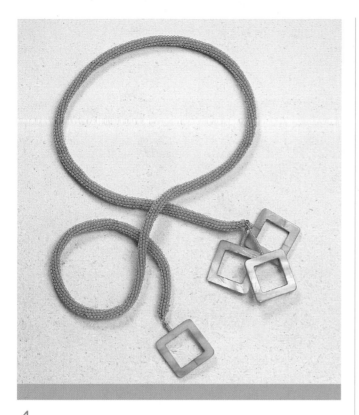

4. Repeat steps 2 and 3 until you've woven a tube that's the length you want for your lariat. When you run out of thread, tie a knot in the old thread between the beads, and weave the end into the beadwork. Start a new thread by weaving it through a few beads in the rope, then tie a knot in the thread, and weave the needle to the place you stopped with the old thread.

5. Thread the squares on head pins, followed by seed beads. Vary the number of seed beads you thread on each head pin to vary the length of the dangles. Use the round-nose pliers to make wrapped loops at the tops of the head pins. Trim any excess wire with the wire cutters.

6. Sew the loops at the ends of the head pins to the ends of the tube. On one end sew three; on the other end sew one. Pass through the loops several times with the needle and thread to secure.

NOTE: You can vary the thickness of your tube by the size beads you use. Just remember to always pick an odd number of beads for making the first circle, and never choose less than nine.

MOTHER-OF-PEARL

Also called nacre, mother-of-pearl is made from the inside of the shells of certain mollusks. Powdered mother-of-pearl was prescribed in Chinese medicine to ease heart palpitations, lower blood pressure, and reduce dizziness. Ancient Sumerian royalty had instruments inlaid with mother-of-pearl, just like rock stars today. The Yaqui Indians of Mexico wear a necklace made of mother-of pearl called the *Hopo'orosim*, which is believed to protect the wearer from evil. Elizabeth I of England gave it its western name.

SILVER BALI BRACELET

BEAD LOVE

ig, bold, and beautiful Bali beads! What better way to wear art on your arm? While you're at it, why not string another for a super fashion statement? (After all, today you can never wear too many bracelets.) The faceted texture of these beads is perfect for creating an earthy ethnic look that will never go out of style.

WHAT YOU NEED

Silver beads, big and small

2 crimp tubes

1 toggle clasp

12 inches (30.5 cm) of flexible beading wire*

Wire cutters

Needle-nose pliers

*This bracelet used the most-flexible wire in a medium thickness

Finished length: 7 inches (17.8 cm)

INSTRUCTIONS

1. Cut the beading wire to length. Thread on a crimp tube, then loop the end of the wire through one end of the toggle clasp. Take the thread back through the crimp. Using needle-nose pliers, crush the crimp flat.

2. String on the beads. Keep in mind that you want to place small beads next to the toggle so it will open and close easily. When you get to the desired length of the bracelet, thread on a crimp tube and loop the wire through the other end of the toggle. Thread the wire back through the crimp, then run the excess wire back through the last few beads. When the beads are secured, crush the crimp and trim the excess wire.

DESIGNER: GEORGIE ANNE JAGGERS

TOO-HOT NECKLACE

All it takes is one focal piece to light the fires of your imagination. The dyed capiz shell sets the tone for this blaze of colors. The design allows you to use a wide assortment of beads from your stash. The interesting use of silk cording adds dimension to the necklace without adding weight.

WHAT YOU NEED

1 focal bead or pendant

Assortment of seed beads

Assortment of beads in a variety of shapes and sizes

Hook-and-eye cone clasp

Size D beading thread

Size 12 beading needle

18 inches (45.7 cm) of ¼-inch (6mm) diameter silk cording

Scissors

Cyanoacrylate glue

Finished length: 15½ inches (39.4 cm)

INSTRUCTIONS

1. Cut a length of thread 5 feet (1.5m) long. Thread it on the needle, doubling it so two threads will pass through the beads. Knot the tails together.

2. Fold the silk cording in half and sew the pendant on, making sure it's secure. Go through the loop of the pendant several times as you sew through the cording. On one side of the cord, begin randomly stringing and sewing seed beads and larger beads to it. Use more seed beads than larger beads.

3. In between each section of beads you string, run the thread through the silk cording and back out. You want to fully embellish the cording, but also leave some of it showing. If you need to change thread during this project, tie off the old thread with a small knot, making it where it won't be seen on the cording, then pass the thread back through some of the beads before cutting off the excess. To add a new thread, knot the thread and enter the cording where you left off.

4. Continue stringing and sewing until you are approximately 1 inch (2.5 cm) from the end of the cording. Sew the tip of the cording shut by passing the thread back and forth through the end. Repeat embellishing and finishing the cord on the other side.

5. Generously apply glue to the inside of one cone on one side of the clasp, then stuff one end of the cording into it. Repeat for the other side. Allow the glue to dry 24 hours before wearing the necklace.

DESIGNER: MOLLY DINGLEDINE

IT'S SIMPLY CHARMING NECKLACE

f charms can be sentimental or meaningful, why not beads? All you intrepid bead lovers have, no doubt, collected some bright and fanciful ones in your travels. This necklace gives you a stylish way to use them so you can recall favorite times and places.

WHAT YOU NEED

Beads—anything goes, as long as it has a hole in it—vintage glass, shell, wood, metal, etc.

Medium- to large-link chain

Head pins

Round-nose pliers

Wire cutters

Liver of sulphur

Finished length: 30 inches (76.2 cm)

INSTRUCTIONS

1. Use the liver of sulphur to oxidize the chain and head pins (see Oxidizing on page 26). This design retains most of the oxidation on the chain to achieve a darker finish that offsets the brightness of the beads.

2. String the beads on the head pins as desired. Using the round-nose pliers, make wrapped loops with one or two wraps for attaching beads that will dangle from the links of chain.

3. Cut the stop off some head pins and string one bead on each. Make wrapped loops at both ends of the bead so you can open the links of the chain and attach the beads to them. Space these beads randomly or evenly to your liking.

4. Have fun attaching beads all the way around the chain until you've used them all. Then, voilà my dear, it's time to go out and turn on the charm.

DESIGNER: NATHALIE MORNU

FLORA, THE RED MENACE BROOCH

BEAD LOVE

Y ou are sure to invite compliments when you wear this piece. The red-on-red brooch shouts, "Aren't I fun and fabulous?" Different types and sizes of beads give the pin texture, while a variety of stringing methods creates the animation that brings it to life.

WHAT YOU NEED

35 red beads of various types and sizes

16 crimp beads

25 head pins

5 tube beads

Pin back, 1¾ inches (4.4 cm) long

12 inches (30.5 cm) of clear, flexible beading wire

24 inches (61 cm) of 24-gauge silver wire

Small file with a smooth round handle

Wire cutters

Round-nose pliers

Finished length: 3½ inches (8.9 cm)

INSTRUCTIONS

1. Open the pin back. Starting at one end of its flat top, wrap the wire tightly around it three times. The coils should lie snugly next to each other, but shouldn't overlap. Next, place the round, smooth handle of the file on the flat top of the pin back. Wrap the wire around the pin back and the handle to make large loops. Slide the file handle out of the way and wrap three more times around just the flat top to make tight coils. Then slide the file back into place to wrap the wire twice around both the pin and the file. Repeat this pattern, alternating three tight coils with two large loops, until the entire length of the pin has been wrapped. Remove the file. Trim the wire if necessary using the wire cutters.

2. String the beads and attach them to the large double loops you made on the pin back. You can use a number of methods for stringing the beads:

- String beads on a head pin, use round-nose pliers to make a wrapped loop, then use needle-nose pliers to attach it to the coils on the pin back.

- String single beads on short lengths of clear, flexible beading wire. Keep the beads in place with crimp beads by stringing a crimp bead, the bead, then another crimp bead. Using a crimp bead, attach the end of the beading wire to the coils.

- Slip beads onto a head pin, add a tube bead, make a loop, and attach it to a coil.

3. Vary the length of the head pins and beading wire to make some beads stand away from the rest of the cluster. Don't be afraid to go all out. The loops you made on the pin back can accommodate lots of beads. Just keep in mind that you want some built-in wiggle room for the clusters because the sense of movement in this brooch is half the fun.

DESIGNER: NANCY KUGEL

Dichroic Glass by Janet Wolery

SHIMMER AND
SHAKE DICHROICS

The irresistible iridescence of the dichroic glass would be enough to make this bracelet and earrings set your fashion favorite. But add the small crystal beads, and you create a bit of movement certain to catch someone's eye.

WHAT YOU NEED

4 rectangular dichroic segments, each approximately ¾ inch (1.9 cm) long, with loops at both ends

2 dichroic segments, each approximately ⅝ inch (1.6 cm) long, with single loops

4 fire-polished 6mm rondelles in a coordinating color

8 silver hill tribe bead caps

56 crystal 4mm bicones

48 silver head pins

6 silver head pins

22-gauge silver wire

Silver toggle clasp

Jump rings

Ear wires of preference

Wire cutters

Round-nose pliers

Finished length: bracelet, 8½ inches (21.6 cm); earrings, 1¼ inches (3.2 cm)

INSTRUCTIONS

Bracelet

1. Lay out your beads. Using the wire cutters, cut four lengths of wire, each long enough to accommodate stringing two bead caps, a 6mm rondelle, and the making of wrapped loops at both ends.

2. String the beads as shown, then use the round-nose pliers to make wrapped loops for attaching them to the dichroic segments. Attach one side of the toggle clasp to each end. You may need to

attach a few jump rings to the bar side of the toggle in order to make the clasp close easily.

3. String the crystal beads on the head pins and attach four to each loop on the dichroic segments using either wrapped or simple loops.

Earrings

1. Cut a length of wire long enough to accommodate stringing one 4mm crystal bead and the making of wrapped loops on both ends.

2. String one crystal bead on the wire. Use the round-nose pliers to make wrapped loops on both ends, attaching one to the loop on the dichroic segment and the other to the loop on the ear wire.

3. String three crystal beads on separate head pins, and attach them to the loop on the dichroic segment using a wrapped or simple loop.

4. Repeat for the other earring.

FELT BEAD NECKLACE
AND EARRINGS

olorful felt beads let you create a soft and funky necklace in no time. Their generous spacing on the silk cord allows each bead to become an individual, free-floating expression of fun. If you want to add a little extra sparkle, as shown in the earrings, randomly space and then sew a few iridescent seed beads to each of the felt beads.

WHAT YOU NEED

1-inch (2.5 cm) diameter felt beads

½-inch (1.3 cm) diameter felt beads

Crimp beads

Pair of ear wires

Iridescent seed beads, optional

Silk beading thread

Sewing needle

Pliers

Awl or straight pin

Scissors

Finished length: necklace 46 inches (116.8 cm); earrings, 2½ inches (6.4 cm)

INSTRUCTIONS

Necklace

1. Cut a generous length of silk thread, slightly longer than the necklace you envision. Lay out your 1-inch (2.5 cm) diameter felt beads on the length of thread to determine how much spacing you want between each bead.

2. Remove the wire-like needle from the end of the silk beading thread. This delicate needle won't be useful when you start threading the beads. Replace that needle with a sewing needle.

3. You may find threading the beads easier with the help of the pliers. Hold the needle with the pliers. Push the needle into the bead until it exits the opposite side, then use the pliers to pull the needle through.

4. Thread one bead onto the silk. Position it in the center. Tie an overhand knot on either side of the bead. Use an awl or straight pin to help you pull the knots up against the bead.

5. Tie a knot where you would like your next bead to sit. Then, thread the needle through the bead and position it up against the knot. Tie a knot on the opposite side of the bead. Continue in this manner until you have threaded beads on one side of the cord. Finish the second side of the cord in the same way.

6. To finish the necklace, thread each of the thread ends through the same bead. Use the thread ends to tie a knot on either side of the bead.

Earrings

1. Knot the end of a length of thread. Thread and knot the ½-inch (1.3 cm) diameter felt beads onto the thread as described for the necklace.

2. Use a crimp bead to attach them to the ear wire or simply knot each thread to the ear wires.

BOLD AS RECYCLED BRASS

Let secondhand jewelry, or jewelry you've grown tired of, be your inspiration. Taking apart an old necklace and redoing it is a great way to recycle the beads you love. The bold size and design of the brass, melon-shaped beads, which had originally been on a dark necklace, were too good to waste. The infusion of natural bone beads, with their wonderful contemporary patterning, gave the old beads new life and inspired the making of matching bracelets.

WHAT YOU NEED

Recycled necklace with melon-shaped brass focus beads

Batik bone beads

African bronze beads

Bone beads

Nylon-coated bead wire

Crimp beads

Toggle clasp

Wire cutters

Crimping pliers

Elastic beading cord

Clear nail polish

Finished length: necklace, 28½ inches (72.5 cm); bracelets, 10 inches (25.4 cm)

INSTRUCTIONS

1. Take apart the recycled jewelry. Set aside the beads you wish to use in your new piece. Save the old beads if they appeal to you. Note: Think before you throw them away—they may be perfect for some future project. If needed, polish or clean any of the beads you're going to use with the appropriate cleaning material.

2. Plan the necklace by laying out the beads on a work surface. This necklace uses a symmetrical and graduated design. When you're satisfied with the design, string the beads on nylon-coated bead wire.

3. Use crimp beads to attach the necklace strand to a simple toggle clasp. Note how the patinated golden color of the clasp works well with the color of the brass beads.

4. For the bracelets, cut 10-inch (25.4cm) lengths of elastic beading cord. String beads on the cord to the desired length for a tight-fitting bracelet. Securely knot the elastic cord and trim the ends. If desired, coat the knot with a small amount of clear nail polish.

AFRICAN GLASS ON NEOPRENE CORD

Beads made of recycled glass are usually heavier than other glass beads because they're solid rather than hollow. Their weight makes choosing the right stringing material especially crucial, particularly if you want to use more than two or three beads in your design. Neoprene cord is a good solution, because it won't sag and will effortlessly hold heavy beads. In addition, neoprene, which comes in a range of contemporary colors, gives any necklace a thoroughly modern look.

WHAT YOU NEED

Recycled glass beads

Neoprene cord

Neoprene O-rings

Short length of silver tubing, approximately ⅝ inch (1.6 cm) long*

Diamond bit and bead reamer or round diamond-coated file

Two-part epoxy

Toothpicks

Scissors

*If you wish to make this necklace with a clasp, use two-part epoxy to attach end caps to the ends of the cord, then attach a clasp of your choosing.

Finished length: 17 inches (43.2 cm); 24 inches (61 cm); 26 inches (66 cm)

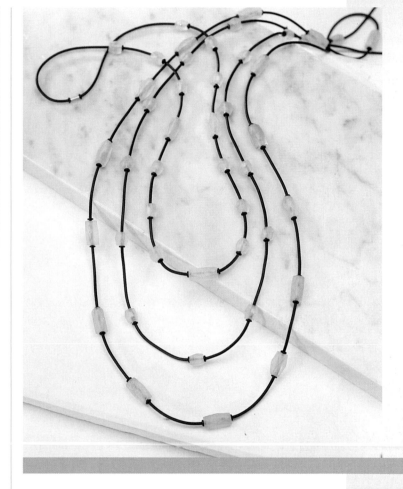

INSTRUCTIONS

1. Check to make sure that your beads will fit onto the cord. If you need to enlarge the holes, use a bead reamer with a diamond tip or a small, round diamond-coated file.

2. Slip a bead onto the cord. Place it in the center. Slip O-rings on either side of the bead to hold it in place.

3. Add more beads to the necklace, securing each with an O-ring on either side of the bead.

4. Trim each end of the neoprene cord to create a flat end. Check to make sure your cord fits snugly in the tubing.

5. Mix up a small amount of two-part epoxy following the manufacturer's directions. Put a dab of epoxy on one end of the cord. Slip one end of the cord halfway into the tubing. Wipe off any excess epoxy. Finish the opposite end of the cord in the same manner. Allow the epoxy to set up before wearing the necklace.

DESIGNERS

Margaret Ashley Amory, a native of Virginia, began beading when she was 12 years old. She graduated from Virginia Tech with concentrations in studio art, English, literature, and creative writing. She currently resides in Asheville, NC, where she makes and sells her jewelry.

Lisa Colby holds a B.F.A. with a concentration in metalsmithing from Wayne State University. She is a self-employed production metalsmith living and working in Asheville, NC. Her work is featured in *1,000 Rings* published by Lark Books. Among her numerous gallery representations are Bellagio Gallery, Asheville, NC; Penland Gallery at the Penland School of Crafts, Penland, NC; and the Signature Shop and Gallery in Atlanta, GA.

Molly Dingledine attended the Savannah College of Art and Design (SCAD) to pursue her love of art and the creative process. After graduation, she moved to Asheville, NC, where she makes jewelry to adorn the body and to express her admiration and fascination for the natural world. She is currently working on a new line of jewelry called Turning Over.

Rachel M. Dow is a jewelry artist who specializes in fabricated sterling, gold, and fine silver metal clay. She received a B.A. in photography and an M.A. in Art Education from California State University at Northridge. When she is not bending and banging metal, she is running around with her four-year-old son and working in fiber. Her work is shown in selected galleries and studios. You can visit her website at www.rmddesigns. com

Cynthia McEwen took a beadmaking class in the summer of 2000, and was hooked. She left her career as a graphic designer and art director in advertising and marketing firms to become a bead artist. You can visit her website at mcewendesign.com

Chris Franchetti is a jewelry artisan and writer living in Seattle, WA. She writes about jewelry and jewelry making for the information site BellaOnline.com and has appeared on several episodes of the show *Jewelry Making* on the DIY Channel. To see some of Chris' jewelry designs, visit www.chettidesigns.com. Links to her writing, including free jewelry projects, can be found on her jewelry portal site, jewelryinfo.net.

Jim Gentry authored *Weekend Crafter Macramé* and was a contributing designer to *The New Macramé,* both published by Lark Books. The primary focus of his current work is knotted jewelry. He is a member of several craft guilds and associations, including Foothills Craft Guild, Tennessee Artist-Craftsmen Association, National Basketry Organization, and is a life member of the Southern Highland Craft Guild. He creates and exhibits his fiber art at Buckhorn Village, an arts and crafts community near Gatlinburg, TN.

Conne Gibson handcrafts unique natural-stone beads, along with her husband Dean, under their company name, Two Cranes. Dean taught Conne her lapidary skills five years ago. Most of their work features stone focal beads. You can visit their website at www.2cranes.biz

Joanna Gollberg is a nationally recognized jeweler, metalsmith, teacher, and writer. Her works have won numerous awards, including one from the American Jewelry Design Council and Pendants Division from Lapidary Journal. Joanna is the author of several books, including *Making Metal Jewelry*, *Creative Metal Crafts*, and *The Art & Craft of Making Jewelry*, all published by Lark Books.

Georgie Anne Jaggers teaches a variety of beading classes and manages a bead store in Asheville, NC. Her work has appeared in *Hippie Crafts* (Lark, 2004) and *Beautiful Beaded Home* (Lark, 2006).

Nancy Kugel, born and raised in St. Louis, MO, has always had an interest in fine crafts, including needlework, basketry, and metalwork. She discovered her love of beading eight years ago, and finds inspiration everywhere she travels. She currenlty lives in Pewaukee, WI, with her husband Reuben, their dog, and two cats.

Bronwynn Lusted followed her husband, Phil McEwan, into making wooden jewelry in 2005 after her 15-year career in the IT industry. Living in Australia, they have a beautiful range of timbers available to them, which provides them with unlimited possibilities for a lifetime of creative jewelry making. They currently sell their work online to people all over the world. You can visit their website at www.banglesofwood.com

Nathalie Mornu works in the editorial department at Lark and has a fascination with shiny things. She has contributed projects to a number of Lark books, including *Decorating Your First Apartment*, *Fun & Fabulous Pillows to Sew*, *Creative Stitching on Paper*, and *Contemporary Bead & Wire Jewelry*.

Rain Newcomb is an avid beader and actress, when she isn't busy working as an editor for Lark Books. She's the author of *The Girls' World Book of Jewelry* and co-author of several more children's books for Lark books.

Thomas Jay Parker specializes in creating one-of-a kind gemstone and cabochon pendants. His work has evolved into silversmithing in which he employs traditional fabrication techniques. When designing beaded necklaces, he enjoys using natural gemstones to create pieces with an organic feel.

Laurie Shaw, designer, works with glass bead artist John Winter under the name Winterglas. Their work is sold in galleries around the country, and has been featured in *Bead and Button*, *Lapidary Journal*, *Beadwork,* and *Bead Unique*. John Winter was recently appointed to the faculty of the Corcoran College of Art and Design in Washington, DC. You can visit their website at www.winterglas.com

Susie Ragland has been wild about beads for a couple of decades, and prefers the chunky and vintage. She lives in Oconomowoc, WI, with her dog Jack and cat Tristan, whose greatest pleasure is lying on Susie's beads when she's trying to work. For more information, visit her at Zowie Beads at windrift@gdinet.com

Darlene Rogalski is a jewelry designer, visual artist, and poet living in Asheville, NC. She seeks to create harmony through asymmetry and color. Using mostly gemstones, she tries to bring nature to her creations. In 2004, her jewelry was shown at the Asheville Gem and Mineral Museum. The name of her jewelry line is *Beadarling*, and can be found at Chevron Trading Post and Bead Company, Asheville, NC.

Terry Taylor is the author and co-author of eight Lark books. When not working on books or projects for books, he's a mixed-media artist and jeweler. He studied jewelry and metal work at John C. Campbell Folk School, Appalachian Center for Crafts, and Haystack Mountain School of Crafts.

INDEX